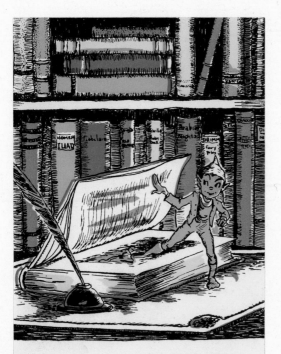

from the books of

Mary H. Stiles

LETTERS TO AN ENTHUSIAST

MARY COWDEN CLARKE

From a drawing by her sister, Emma Novello.

LETTERS TO AN ENTHUSIAST

By MARY COWDEN CLARKE

Being a Series of Letters addressed to ROBERT BALMANNO, ESQ., *of New York, 1850–1861. Edited by* ANNE UPTON NETTLETON

WITH TEN PHOTOGRAVURE PLATES

CHICAGO · A. C. McCLURG & CO. PUBLISHERS · *MDCCCCII*

PREFATORY NOTE

NO apology is needed for offering to the public the following hitherto unpublished letters of Mary Cowden Clarke, who, added to her fame as a writer, has the twofold distinction of being the daughter and the sister of illustrious musicians, and the wife of an accomplished *littérateur*. Among her letters this modest fragment was found :

" Mary Victoria Novello was a quiet, retiring child, plainish in person, simple in manner; and she advanced from girlhood to womanhood without giving token of possessing any distinguishing talent, among a generally gifted family. But she enjoyed the advantage of meeting, during her growth, some of the chief writers of the day, and this consociation stimulated her natural intelligence into literary attempts that took the shape of papers on various subjects, which appeared in print while the writer was in her fifteenth year."

On July 5, 1828, she married Charles Cowden Clarke, a lecturer, critic, and author, who had reckoned Keats as his intimate friend, whose

daily associates were Charles Lamb, Douglas Jerrold, William Hazlitt, Leigh Hunt, William
Godwin, and other notable writers.

To him Keats wrote:

> "I have long time been my fancy feeding
> With hopes that you one day would think the reading
> Of my rough verses not an hour misspent."

Also:

> "You first taught me all the sweets of song."

Fully twenty years younger than her husband,
Mrs. Clarke, as a girl, had not been present at
the after-performance suppers when Dowton, Liston, Bannister, Elliston, and Lamb's sweetheart,
Fanny Kelly, met; but as time went on, from
being merely a child in the eyes of Charles
Clarke, she grew to claim a place with him, first
as a comrade, then as his heart's desire, and so
was permitted to make merry with these gifted
friends. The intercourse between the Novellos,
Hunts, and Lambs was close and full of innocent
pleasure. No wonder Charles Lamb, after one
of these suppers, called back when leaving,
"You're very nice people!" For this circle
loved C. C. C., or "Three Hundred," as Leigh

Hunt dubbed Charles Cowden Clarke and his wife, and their friendship endured until they were separated by death.

It was in the home of Vincent Novello that Mrs. Shelley and Jane Williams sought rest and sympathy after the poet's tragic death.

When visiting Charles and Mary Lamb, and while wandering in their flower garden, Mrs. Clarke first determined to undertake the task of compiling a Concordance to Shakespeare, and to this work she gave sixteen years of her life.

Mrs. Clarke was deeply gratified on learning that the service done by her to all lovers of Shakespeare was fully appreciated in America. A Mr. Robert Balmanno admired her so sincerely that he wrote to Douglas Jerrold, begging him to ask Mrs. Clarke to send him one of the slips used in preparing the Concordance, that he might have a word in her own handwriting, and jocularly proposed sending two ounces of California gold in acknowledgment thereof. She graciously complied with his request, and in return he sent her two gold pens. Mr. Balmanno then moved to enthusiasm some of the most prominent persons in America, and a number of these — among them Daniel Webster, William Cullen Bryant, Richard Grant White, Henry Wadsworth Longfellow, Charlotte Cushman, and S. Austin Allibone — unitedly sent to Mrs. Clarke a testimonial in the shape of a large rosewood chair. From this began a correspondence which lasted eleven years; and though during this time Mr. Balmanno and Mrs. Clarke never saw each other, it ceased only at his death, in 1861. Mention is made of this friendship and correspondence in the essay on Douglas Jerrold, and in chapter ninth of Mr. and Mrs. Clarke's delightful book, " Recollections of Writers."

These letters breathe so sweet a spirit, and are a revelation of such a winning personality, that they throw new light on an author who persistently veiled her individuality, and whose intense modesty often concealed the loveliness of her character and the charity of her heart, content as she was in the approving love of her family and friends. They are written in so fine and delicate a hand as to be almost illegible without a magnifying glass. The first letter is addressed simply:

PREFATORY NOTE

" *To The American Enthusiast,*
                    New York City."

And it reached its destination through the courtesy of the postal officials.

Charles Cowden Clarke lived to the age of ninety, and his wife, having spent over forty years in the Riviera, died at the Villa Novello, Genoa, January 12, 1898, aged eighty-eight. Mrs. Clarke's mind remained clear and vigorous to the end of her " Long Life," and her home was the object of many a pilgrimage, for she was a link that bound the literary culture of the close of the century with its beginning. Percy Fitzgerald wrote : " At this moment I do not know of any one now alive who had known or spoken to Charles Lamb. . . . It is a pleasant thing, however, to have talked with his friends, and to have pressed hands that have shaken his. The Cowden Clarkes are dead."

ANNE UPTON NETTLETON.

February 1, 1902.

LIST OF ILLUSTRATIONS

LETTERS TO AN ENTHUSIAST

FEBRUARY 18TH, 1850,
CRAVEN HILL COTTAGE, BAYSWATER.

DEAR " ENTHUSIAST ":

FOR I am not quite sure whether I ought to address you as Sir or Madam, though I incline to the former.— I should have sooner acknowledged the receipt of your most kind letter of the 22nd of January but that I waited until the arrival of the precious " little parcel " should enable me to write to you with your own dainty gift, the gold pen.

Through the kind courtesy of Mr. Crofton Croker it has at length reached me, having been detained at the Liverpool Custom House to be examined. As it was opened there, it may be as well to state the contents of the packet, that you may know whether it has reached me in the state you desired it should : An elegantly ornamented card box, containing a smaller one of crimson velvet, in which were six gold pens; a holder of ivory and silver; another of tortoise-shell and silver; the whole

[15]

enveloped in a mat of dove-coloured cloth and
rose-coloured satin. Really, the enumeration of
all these elegancies is like a sentence from the
Arabian Nights describing a gift presented by
some prince to a princess, at least; while the
distance they have travelled seems to endue
them with as wondrous properties as any of the
marvels therein mentioned, a steam voyage
across the Atlantic between January 2nd and
February 7th seeming almost as miraculous as
a trip on the magic square of carpet or a flight
in Aladdin's Palace. Accept my warm thanks
for bestowing such a beautiful gift upon myself,
while your kindness is enhanced by having
enabled me to share it with my husband, who
desires me to add his acknowledgments to mine.
He has selected the tortoise-shell pen, while I
have the ivory one.

But now to your obliging letter. I should be
sorry to impugn the veracity of your informant.
The only American gentlemen that I remember
to have spent an evening with are your distinguished countryman, Emerson; Dr. Wain-
wright, of Boston; Mr. Lowell Mason, also of
Boston; and Mr. James Hall, Jr., of New York
—all possessed of far too excellent judgment
and good sense to commit any such mistake.
But the gentleman who described me to you

as "a lovely darling" (I can't help laughing as I write the words) must have spent the evening in question with me some (well, I won't say how many) years ago, when I was a baby of a few months old, and on that occasion happened *not* to be crying or screaming; under which circumstances all babies may be fairly called lovely darlings, however homely-featured they may chance to be. At no other period of my existence could the epithet be applied with propriety to one who is as plain a woman, short of absolute ugliness (though even this clause, to any less partial being than my mother or husband, might seem to savour of self-delusion), as you can well picture to yourself. As near an idea to the truth, perhaps, as you can receive on this point is conveyed in those words which my friend Mr. Douglas Jerrold — in "Punch" for Dec. 11th, 1847 — has put into the mouth of Shakespeare's wife, touching the individual in question, and her personal appearance.

I have been thus frank in endeavouring to convey to you a correct impression about myself, in order that I may set you an example, and induce you to tell me somewhat concerning the identity of "The American Enthusiast." I have already found out much from the Enthusiast's own communication: I have discovered that the Enthusiast is not young, inasmuch as there is mention of "the course of a long life;" I have also discovered that the Enthusiast is munificent, inasmuch as a few lines were deemed worthy of such rich acknowledgment; I perceive likewise that the Enthusiast has delicacy, inasmuch as there is manifest a desire to lessen rather than augment the merit of his gift, in speaking of its intrinsic value; I find that the Enthusiast has affectionate sentiment, by the mention of my husband; and there is also traceable veneration for sacred parent-love, in the allusion to my beloved mother. The Enthusiast's kindliness of nature will probably be gratified to learn that the pleasure afforded by the letter from New York was shared with this beloved mother, a copy of it having been transcribed in my long gossip-letter written weekly to Nice, where my father and mother at present reside, the climate being peculiarly suited to the latter's delicate state of health.

In reply to your obliging offer of American autographs, I own that the one of which I feel at present most anxious to become possessed is the genuine one — the real signature — of "The American Enthusiast." I should feel it an additional obligation to those already conferred on me by that personage if I might be favoured with a knowledge of how to address, and how transmit, a parcel, so as to ensure its reaching that hand, should I at some future time fulfil my hope of sending a printed copy of a book on which I am at present engaged, which I flatter myself may prove of interest, and the MS. of which shall be continued thenceforth written with the Enthusiast's golden gift.

But let me conclude this long epistle, — into which the pleasant novelty of holding converse across the Atlantic has beguiled me, — by requesting you to accept my earnest thanks for your kind letter and beautiful present, and to believe that I must remain, dear Enthusiast,

Your most obliged and grateful
MARY COWDEN CLARKE.

" The American Enthusiast,"
New York.

The following is the only letter in the collection written to Mrs. Clarke by Mr. Balmanno.

NEW YORK, 2ND APRIL, 1850.

DEAR MADAM:

BY the kind attention of our postmaster your very kind letter dated the 18th February reached me quite safe. I need hardly describe the glow of real pleasure it afforded me; I am sure you can suppose it. Ever since the publication of your unrivalled Concordance I have considered you, in common with thousands, one of the most estimable and extraordinary women that ever existed, certainly as exhibiting the most wonderful instincts of female perseverance ever heard of. I may say with truth that, next to Shakespeare, I worship you. I had had an ardent desire ever since the publication of your glorious work to possess one of the little slips on which you wrote the sentences, and although I now possess what is ten times more valuable, I am not quite sure that my original desire is even yet quite extinguished. I wish it to adorn the volume, and to show and explain the way in which the wonderful work was worked out. I have understood that you had a basket or a box for each letter of the alphabet, and that the lines were deposited in the boxes until the whole of each play was completed. From a very simple calculation, I make about three hundred and ten thousand lines — a number perfectly astounding. If I had not already intruded much too far on your kindness and time, it would be very, very gratifying to know from yourself whether the above is anything like the process by which you proceeded, and whether it was not owing to the sweet endearing kindness and encouragement of your beloved husband that you did not often give up in despair. I was once told by one who knew Lord Byron and his sister, that when sitting one evening, his Lordship was seized with one of his fits of inspiration, and solicited his sister to write while he composed; and he went on, throwing out the most glorious flashes of his genius, he walking backwards and forwards, until very late in the night. She felt quite exhausted and told him she could go on no longer, when he went up and caressed her in the kindest manner, called her his own dear Augusta, and implored her to go on, as otherwise if he stopped he could never resume the strain. I unfortunately forgot to ask which of his poems it was. I can easily suppose that but for equal kindness on the part of Mr. Clarke, you would have broken down in your gigantic labour. Many, many things are crowding on my imagination, and I am afraid I am going to bore you with a very long and very foolish letter. Pray, therefore, throw it aside, until some moment of lassitude in the afternoon, when an anodyne to sleep would be acceptable.

First, I must give you a settler as to the correctness of the term which my friend applied to your personal appearance. It was none of the gentlemen you named, but one whom I think you would allow to be a better judge; but in fact one of those you named fully bears out the

appellation, and so you see there are two to one
against you. But you must be made to understand, dear madam, that my American phrases
bear a somewhat different interpretation to what
they do in England. Thus with us, "a lovely
woman" almost invariably alludes to sweetness
of disposition, kindness, amiability, gentleness
of manner, absence of affectation or arrogance.
The most beautiful face in the world would not
with us be lovely unless the owner had qualities of mind and manner, but when with these
qualities — which I now know you possess in an
eminent degree — there is added enough of personal charms to make a lady very agreeable to
look at and speak to, she is not only a lovely
woman, but a lovely darling! Ergo, you *are* a
lovely darling; my friend was perfectly correct.
I'd buckler that against a million! and Mr.
Clarke should be my second. You are doubtless
aware there are many other words and phrases
which have a meaning here altogether different
from what they do in England; *e. g.* a *clever*
fellow is merely one who is kind, obliging, and
good-natured; an ugly fellow may be a very handsome man, — it alludes to disposition; and "a
fine man" may also be humpbacked. Ugliness
and fineness in men pertains to qualities of mind
and manner. I think I've said enough to turn

the laugh from the left to the right side of the mouth.

I have looked at the passage in " Punch." Mr. Jerrold is a keen observer, exact truth to nature is in all he says. Many years ago, while resident in London, I observed an elegantly dressed young couple stop opposite a bookseller's window, where the portrait of a beautiful creature was exhibited in one of the new annuals. " By Jove, what a beautiful, what a lovely face ! " said the gentleman. " Oogh, I see nothing so very beautiful," said the bride, with a toss of her bonnet, walking him off. The portrait was after one of Lawrence's superlative faces — a Miss Thayer. I mentioned it to him; he laughed and said, " The sex all over." He was my informant respecting Lord Byron and Mrs. Leigh, his sister.

If you will try not to laugh I will relate to you the most extraordinary and ecstatic dream I ever had in my life; and will you believe me, when I assure you most solemnly, that it was about Shakespeare and his wife ? It occurred on the night between the 10th and 11th of February. Could there be any mysterious connection between it and what you must have been meditating writing about ? My dream indicated no particular place, but I thought it was in a good-sized

[23]

handsome room. He was dressed almost exactly in the same costume represented in the small statuette. He stood with his back towards the fireplace. There was a good-humoured smile on his face, almost inclining to a laugh. Oh! I can never forget it. Anne was sitting, and what surprised me was to see her, a large woman, not fat, but of a tall large frame — good-looking, handsome, with very fine large gray eyes. I can see her still; but I thought she had the most superb bust I ever beheld, white as a lily, but exquisitely round and full, as that of the Venus herself. There was rather a display of it, and I could seldom keep my eyes off. Shakespeare was going out to some party or dinner, and Anne exhibited a few whiffs of jealousy. He did not once speak, but she was speaking to him — and in poetry! Yes, excellent poetry, as it seemed; every couplet told exactly. I was in a perfect delirium of delight. Her words came so freely, so distinctly, I thought they were enchanting. He kept smiling on, and she kept rhyming, and I awoke mad with happiness and delight. Her words were fresh in my memory, fixed as I thought for life; but having a thousand times imagined I too composed in my dreams, and awakened still rhyming and believing I could recall, and always been disappointed, I determined on this occasion in-

stantly to write down at least ten or twelve lines.
I leaped up and ran to the mantel for a match to
light our spirit lamp. I groped, but found no
match. Then I ran into the front bedroom and
found one, but broke it on the bar of the grate.
Then I recalled that the scroll of my Journal of
the weather, on foolscap, lay open on the bureau;
tumbled out my pencil, and thought that by
writing large and far apart I could manage to
make it out in daylight. As soon as morning
dawned I got up and went to my Journal, and —
horror of horrors! I had written on a piece of
well-blotted blotting paper, and all I could find
on the white paper was the commencement of
one line, and the last two — the very lines which
woke me up. Her words were intended as a sort
of injunction how to behave or conduct himself
at the party. The few words of one line were,
"Waste not time in —" The concluding couplet was:

> "Only let me charge thee this,
> That thou dost not even kiss!"

And this is the amount of my never-to-be-
forgotten Shakespeare dream. Reverting to
dreams, I will enclose the copy of a few lines
by my inestimable wife, my darling little Mary,
which she threw into verse the very morning
after it occurred. As it relates to her mother,

whom she idolizes, I can fancy — if you think there is any merit in it — it will be acceptable to your own feelings, loving a dear mother as affectionately as my sweet Mary loves hers. Would you like to hear a bit of romance?

AUGUST 4TH, 1850,
CRAVEN HILL COTTAGE, BAYSWATER.

DEAR SIR:

I FEEL terribly in arrears with you, when I find how many kind communications from you I have to acknowledge. But in this matter you have also shown your kindness, by promising you will forgive me should I not answer as much at length as you in truth deserve. Let me thank you, in summary, for your letters of 11 and 17 June, and for their obliging manifold contents; also for the two books of prints and the very entertaining Magazine articles. Your dear wife's verses charm me very much; they contain some exquisite music. How very amiable and generously trustful of you to send your two lovely little " Leanders " forth upon the waters of the Atlantic! But your best reward for such kindness will be, I trust, the assurance that the sight of them gave both Charles and myself

[26]

great delight. They are eminently tasteful in design.

Will you not think it strange that, although Leigh Hunt is an idol of ours, and although we live but little more than two miles distance from his present residence, yet that we seldom see him? We live quite a hermit life here in the cottage, visiting very little. I shall therefore not longer detain your two etchings in the hope of being able to show them to Mr. Hunt, as I feel how probable it is that such an occasion might be some time in arriving. I therefore enclose them herewith, trusting that they may perform their transit in all safety. I have somewhere seen it quoted from Montaigne that " the arms of friendship are long enough, and join hands from one end of the world to the other." In your kind thought of sending these little etchings across the ocean, I have felt a wonderful realization of the genial old Frenchman's sayings. Because Charles saw you looking at that " Leander " one morning many years ago, that you should have sent it to meet our eyes once more is certainly a piece of sentiment with such a force in it as to amount to a grasp of the hand, and as such we felt it and welcomed it, and now reciprocate it in spirit. Imagine, my dear sir — you have vivid imagination enough, and enthusiasm

[27]

enough, I know — that Charles and Mary Cowden Clarke are giving you a warm shake of the hand at this moment.

I feel extremely proud of what you tell me respecting Mr. Washington Irving's opinion; but with all my respect for that name, — and I assure you it is a very sincere one, — I must still adhere to my own judgment in the matter. "Like a woman," I am afraid you will exclaim — " wilful, and not very rational." Forgive me, but let the letter in question remain unpublished. Permit me also, once more, to put your enthusiastic scruples at rest at once and forever about the MS. pages, by whispering in your ear that for the last several months, whenever the housemaid has wanted paper to light the fires, she has fetched a basketful from a certain dismantled summer house where the MS. of the Concordance has lain ever since its author had the gratification of knowing it was stereotyped, printed, and published. Thus you see, dear sir, that the obliging importance you give to the few pages you have, by offering to return them to me should I wish to make the MS. complete, is entirely unnecessary. It is only your own enthusiasm which could attach any such value to them.

Having told you what a hermit life we lead,

[28]

Charles and myself living with my brother in my father's house, — the mere cottage its name proclaims, — ever since the latter joined my mother in Nice, seeing no company and visiting little, you will not wonder that we should be unable to show Mr. and Mrs. Dyer the hospitable attentions we could desire ; but at the same time, should they do us the favour to think it worth while to call here, so far from London, we should be most happy to see any friends of yours.

With Mr. Clarke's and my own kind remembrances to Mrs. Balmanno and yourself, believe me to be

Yours faithfully,
MARY COWDEN CLARKE.

JANUARY 1ST, 1851,
CRAVEN HILL COTTAGE, BAYSWATER.

DEAR ENTHUSIAST :

HOW can I sufficiently thank you for the extremely kind and friendly interest you have evinced in my behalf, and for the personal exertion you have taken to secure the advantage of my book in America ? I can but say I am deeply sensible of them, and more than ever of the vast debt of gratitude I owe to the beloved name of Shakespeare.

[29]

Your account of the " Record " amused us all immensely. As I read your droll description of the first era since the creation, I could not help thinking of that exquisitely humorous bit in Racine's admirable — alas, only — comedy, " Les Plaideurs," where a gentleman in commencing a narration begins with " Avant la naissance du monde," and the other interrupts him with " Ah, passons au deluge ! "

After what you say in your last letter, about the delight you take in the design you have in hand, I dare not tell you your own feelings in the matter. But ah, you naughty Enthusiast, you clearly showed, by your deprecating any remonstrance on my part when you first announced the intention, how truly you knew what must naturally be my dismay upon hearing of such a thing, which only an enthusiasm amounting to fanaticism such as Mrs. Balmanno and I know where to look for could have thought of.   You ask forgiveness for a hasty expression you say you dropped in first speaking of this subject.   I presume you refer to your allusion to the Prince of Darkness, who we are told on good authority is a gentleman.   To show you how little need there was for an apology, I will tell you what I said when I came to your mention of his Highness : " Of course my Enthusiast will not let the D——l drive him from his purpose, if he will not let her whom he has so often called an angel prevail."

You were surprised to find my brother Alfred call me Victoria. It is my second Christian name, but by my own family I am still called Vicky, Victoria, and all possible variations of that regal cognomen. Leigh Hunt used to call me "Victorinella." You make my letters terribly egotistical, perforce, my dear sir, by all your friendly questions. We, the Trihominate, had the privilege of being present yesterday morning at a lecture delivered by Edward Cowper, on and in the works of the Great Exhibition Crystal Palace. It was a most interesting morning. All the scientific men of London (nay, many came up from the provinces) were present. The building itself formed the best illustration of the lecture, though there were excellent models of all the details, as the lecturer successively explained them. Mr. Cowper is an admirable lecturer, so clear, so easy, so familiar in his style. And his knowledge of his subjects is so masterful that he enables the most unscientific of his audience to comprehend his explanations. After the lecture, which did not extend beyond an hour, we examined every portion of the work; and it was extremely interesting to see the actual progress of each department: the circular saws for the sash-bars; the drilling apparatus; the glazing wagon in which two men are seated, and which travels on small wheels along the roof covered with light tarpaulins, beneath which the glaziers put in the panes of glass. Every pane of glass is brought there of a precise size; every column of iron is exactly measured before it arrives, so that the workmen have nothing to do but to place each compartment in its proper position and adjust them together. The edifice is of such magnitude that trains of timber and iron, drawn by teams of horses, look like toys there; men cling to the roof, like spiders or flies. Several large elm trees are enclosed within the structure, as we cockneys did not like some of our favourite old giants of the Park to be hewn down. The lecturer made a pleasant allusion to the persistence with which John Bull had preserved the Trees of Liberty, in contra-distinction to the short duration of those of our more volatile neighbours, the French. They ought to be truly pointed to as standing proofs of the might of public opinion in England.

I suppose you see Leigh Hunt's Journal. Is it not delightful to find his ever-young poet heart and mind continuing to dispense enjoyment to his readers? You have doubtless also seen the Christmas number of " Household Words." The " Christmas Tree" paper is charming, is it not?

But nothing can console me for the cessation of his monthly " Two Leaves." I think his " Copperfield " (though it is difficult to choose among such admirable productions for the best) is the very finest thing C. D. has done. You must know he is one of my idols. But whose is he not ?

The Trihominate desire their united kindest regards to the dear Enthusiast. The least worthy member begs you will believe her to be

Yours faithfully,
MARY COWDEN CLARKE.

It gives me great joy to find you like " Portia."

FEBRUARY 7TH, 1851,
CRAVEN HILL COTTAGE, BAYSWATER.

DEAR SIR :

I AM your debtor for two most kind and pleasant letters; but I am your debtor for so many proofs of friendly regard, that I can but comfort myself with the reflection that you know, as well as I, who it is that says " Thanks, to men of noble minds, is honourable meed; " [1] and thanks I offer you most warmly and sincerely.

Your account of the Brooklyn Hawthorns was particularly interesting, and also that of your

---

[1] " Titus Andronicus," Act I, Scene I.

3 [33]

keeping holiday with your Mary on the first of
May. For many years my Charles has been in
the habit of reading Milton's fine hymn annually,
on that morning, alone to me. It is rather a
singular coincidence that you as a child formerly
frequented Kensington Gardens with your aunt,
and so did I. My mother's sister made a pet
of me then, and used to take me with her there
for a long walk. I remember thinking the West
Walk there quite the end of the world.

You made us laugh very heartily about the
" bam " you played off respecting those exquisite
cedar articles under pretext of their being for the
" *Fair*," and vaunting your Victoria as worth a
million of Prince Alberts! My men-folk — and
they ought to know — are highly amused at the
visionary excellencies with which you invest
M. C. C. If ever you fulfil your intention of
alighting from the balloon at Craven Hill, alas!
you will then find how fatally the Enthusiast has
allowed his imagination to run away with him.
He has dressed up a commonplace sort of a
person in all kinds of delightful attributes, and
Pygmalion-like, has fallen in love with his own
creation.

Although I have so lightly alluded above to
your beautiful present of the cedar tubs, etc., do
not think I esteem lightly your kind generosity.

Accept my grateful thanks for them, and for
your goodness. I will hope that ere they arrive
you will explicitly tell me your own wishes on
the subject of presenting one to Mrs. Crofton
Croker. There will still be another for my
sister Emma, which I shall assuredly give her
when she comes to England, telling her all the
history of it and its kind donor. She is at
present at Rome; she has the charge of Mr.
Roll's daughters. Having been for some years
in Italy, travelling with my sister Clara,[1] she is
peculiarly fitted for the undertaking she is at
present engaged in.

You say you "wonder what sort of winter we
have at Bayswater." Wonderfully mild, no snow
worth mentioning; a good deal of rain, and the
winds are very blustering (alas! I often think of
the poor Atlantic steamers during those bois-
terous nights); but no piercing cold, no frost.

I should like to know what is the word you
somehow dislike in " Portia." Not having the
"Yankee edition " as you call it, I cannot ascertain; so tell me.

You speak in your own " Enthusiast " style
about my editing a Folio Shakespeare. It would
be a great glory, but where am I to find an

---

[1] Clara Anastasia Novello, the famous songstress, married in
1843 to Count Gigliucci, an Italian nobleman.

Enthusiast among publishers who would think of undertaking such a work? No, no, dear sir; I fear few possess your exalted notions on this subject. I acknowledge the safe receipt of Mr. Putnam's agreement. A thousand thanks for all the trouble and kind interest you have taken in this affair.

I always thought it probable you might come over to England this Exhibition year, when all the World and his Wife are visiting the dear little Island. Why trust to a balloon? Come in a vessel. Though I am very much of Dr. Johnson's opinion that "no man who has ingenuity enough to get into jail would ever think of going to sea;" yet I must say, I think steamers less "vain things for safety" than balloons, so I shall expect to see you drop in upon the Trihominate some of these fine May mornings, as you promised.

The "Two Leaves" I alluded to, of Charles Dickens, are those he allows us to hope for in his preface to Copperfield. More dear monthly green-covered numbers of his enchanting stories. I idolize him in his long stories. There he is perfectly inimitable.

Yes, I had the pleasure of meeting admirable Miss Kelly at beloved Charles Lamb's house in Russell Square once, and once when he lived

at Enfield Chase. Her acting, especially of comedy, was such as I never expect to behold again. But we live quite hermit lives, and I have given up theatres, and most amusements that involve late hours. If I can find time before this goes off, I will try and write out a notice of Miss Kelly, which I had the pleasure of writing for a friend who wanted to give an article in the Manchester paper on her acting, but not having been a playgoer in her time himself, and knowing I was a great admirer of hers, asked me to write one. I hope it will remind you of some touches in her plays that will awaken a sympathy on that score between us, as well as many points on which I flatter myself we have the same tastes. Forgive this scribble. But I can't emulate a certain friend of mine who can write *well* as well as small. Give him my love — I mean my regards, Mrs. Balmanno.

Believe me to be, dear sir and Enthusiast,

Your grateful

M. C. C.

The following is the notice of Miss Kelly referred to in the above letter.

" We have already had the pleasure of announcing to our readers that they will shortly have an opportunity of seeing and hearing this gifted artist, who is about to visit Manchester, where she will give a series

of readings from Shakespeare, at the Athenæum.
Those who are fortunate enough to have witnessed the
performances of this admirable actress on the stage
will readily believe that her delivery of the greatest
dramatic writing that was ever penned must prove
a high intellectual enjoyment. We know that Charles
Lamb — no mean authority — says of her:

> ' You are not, Kelly, of the common strain
>   That stoop their pride and female honour down,
> To please that many-headed beast, *the Town*,
>   And vend their lavish smiles and tricks for gain ;
> By fortune thrown amid the actors' train
>   You keep your native dignity of thought ;
> The plaudits that attend you come unsought,
>   As tributes due unto your natural vein.
> Your tears have passion in them, and a grace
>   Of genuine freshness, which our hearts avow ;
> Your smiles are winds whose ways we cannot trace,
>   That vanish and return we know not how —
> And please the better from a pensive face,
>   A thoughtful eye, and a reflecting brow.'

"These lines contain not merely the eulogium of
partial friendship, but they convey a true impression
of Miss Kelly's style. Her manner was eminently
sensible, as well as imaginative; carefully polished, as
well as easy and graceful; pregnant with meaning,
as well as buoyant and animated. Her acting was
instinct with thought and feeling; her by-play was apt,
original, and suggestive; while her voice was exquisitely melodic in its tones, flexible, earnest, and capable
of the most varied expressions — from the tremulous
emotion of pathos and the passionate cadence of grief,
to the playful intonation of sly sarcasm and the exu-

berant ringing laughter of broad farce. Who that
remembers her saucy servant-maidism, her pert replies
to her old master, her dawdling, worrying delays when
he bids her to begone; her awkward scattering of the
contents of her pocket — the tumblings out of brass
thimble, shiny apple, nutmeg-grater, charmed cramp-
bone, rolling penny-pieces, etc. etc., with the scrambling futility of her endeavours to restrain and regain
them, in the part of Patch in 'The Busybody,' can
wonder that Lord Byron used to go and see her every
time she played the character? Who that can recall
the impudent hardness of her manner when hinting for
a gratuity, in the part of some servant girl, in the farce
of 'Free and Easy;' the roguish cheatery, with the
fine-lady airs, of her Betty Finikin; the subtle mixture
of genuine touches of feminine tenderness with the
bold, unabashed freedom of a Newgate education,
that distinguished her Lucy in 'The Beggar's Opera,'
can fail to recognize in her the true zest of comedy?
We will confess that her comic vein had always greater
charms for us than even her serious one, good as that
undoubtedly was. For who that witnessed the exquisite tact of her by-play, the heart-beating agitation of
her utterance, the unconscious pertinacity and conscious timidity of her glances, their alternate lingering
and withdrawal, in her portraiture of a young girl sud-
denly yielding to the influence of a first love, but must
allow her power of depicting passion and sentiment?
It was a slight sketch, — a character in a little piece
taken from one of Grattan's stories, — and it is some
years since we beheld the performance; but the mode

in which the actress embodied the slender outline, the
simple attitude in which she sat at the table watching
the young officer, as he partakes of the refreshment
with which she has provided him in a moment of peril,
the look of absorbed interest, the drinking of love,
as it were into her very being with each moment, the
flattering tones, the unconscious replies, the abstracted
manner, the mechanical action of the fingers, the
absent way in which she plaited the tablecloth before
her into minute folds, — a touch worthy of ranking
beside that one of Richardson's, where he makes Charlotte Grandison place the tip of her little finger in the
centre of her diamond ring, while she spins it round and
round upon the table during her vexed colloquy with
her brother, — all these minutiæ of detail arise vividly
before our mind's eye, composing a finished dramatic
picture, and testifying the skill of the actress. We
were never so fortunate as to see Miss Kelly play the
part alluded to in Charles Lamb's sonnet, ' To a Celebrated Performer in *The Blind Boy ;*' but the memory
we retain of her Emmeline in 'King Arthur' — also
a representation of quenched vision — enables us to
recognize the accuracy of this other tribute of his to
her genius:

> ' Rare artist ! who, with half thy tools or none,
>   Canst execute with ease thy curious art,
> And press thy powerful'st meanings on the heart
>   Unaided by the eye, expression's throne!
> While each blind sense, intelligential grown
>   Beyond its sphere, performs the effect of sight ;
> Those orbs alone, wanting their proper might,
>   All motionless and silent seemed to moan

The unseemly negligence of Nature's hand,
   That left them so forlorn. What praise is thine,
O mistress of the passions ; artist fine !
   Who dost our souls against our sense command,
Plucking the horror from a sightless face,
   Lending to blank deformity a grace.'

" While indulging ourselves with the above reminiscences, — for her name is associated with the most delightful of our play-going days, — we found ourselves, alas, speaking in the past tense when enumerating some of the excellencies that mark this accomplished artist's style; but as the stage has been for some time deprived of their lustre, and as we can no longer hope to enjoy them there, we the rather congratulate ourselves and our readers on the prospect of a new field where we may witness their display — in Miss Kelly's Readings from Shakespeare. November, 1848."

FEBRUARY 12TH, 1851,
CRAVEN HILL COTTAGE, BAYSWATER.

DEAR ENTHUSIAST :

BY a mistake, the accompanying letter was not posted in time for the last mail. I can scarcely regret this now, since it allows me the opportunity of acknowledging the receipt of the American copy of " Portia." Many thanks to you, my dear sir. The word in the tenth line from the foot, page 22, which I presume you object to, is "starchedly." Now, my dear sir, Addison — allowed to be a model of style —

[41]

uses the word in this sense: "This professor is to infuse into their manners that beautiful political *starch*, which may qualify them for levees, conferences, and visits." Swift, a master in style, has: "Does the Gospel anywhere describe a *starched* squeezed countenance, a stiff, formal gait, or a singularity of manners?"

Enthusiast. Ay, ay; this is all very well, M. C. C., but Addison and Swift, though both classical writers, are not classics of the Shakespearean era.

M. C. C. But Ben Jonson — he is one of the Elizabethans — has a passage that bears me out, I think. He says —

Enthusiast. Oho! Mrs. C. C.! I see whereabouts you are. You are trying to knock me on the head with Dr. Johnson; braining me with "the great Lexicographer"; belabouring, cudgelling, "thwacking me with the distaff" of Johnsonian authorities, citations, and quotations, in order that I may be "banged into dumbness."

M. C. C. Nay, but I assure you, my dear Enthusiast, that —

Enthusiast. Well, well; have it as you will, "darling." To please you, I'll even say with the clown in "Antony and Cleopatra," "The word's a good word; I wish ye joy of the word!"

M. C. C. Indeed, I am not anxious about my word, only —

Enthusiast. No, no, I see; you are not anxious about your word; only, like a true woman, resolved to have the last word.

M. C. C. Pardon me, I would merely —

Enthusiast. Ah! Ha! Ha!

M. C. C. Just this —

Enthusiast. Ah! Ha!

M. C. C. One word —

Enthusiast. The last? Ah, ha, ha, ha, ha, ha, ha!

—Atlantic echoes the roar —

M. C. C. (stopping her ears). I am stunned. I give up the point.

Enthusiast. Bravissima! Right woman still! even in yielding, she persists. Against Ocean itself she 'll retort; a very Partington of pertinacity!

———

FEBRUARY 27, 1851,
CRAVEN HILL COTTAGE, BAYSWATER.

DEAR ENTHUSIAST:

HOW am I to thank you for your superb present? The cedar chest arrived in safety; and as we unpacked it and I beheld the magnitude as well as beauty of your gift, I really felt half ashamed to accept so handsome a present. But the very care with which each article was arranged, the sweet-scented shavings, the muslin bags to put them in, all bespoke so much kindness and interest on the part of the donor as to make me feel just that assurance of liking and affectionate partiality which reconciles one to accepting the most generous and munificent gifts from relations, or very dear friends. Let me thank you then, dear sir, as one of the latter. For although our acquaintance dates back no very long time, yet in that space you have contrived to bestow upon me so many proofs of regard that you live in my thoughts constantly, as one of my dearest and kindest friends; and yet, thank God, I can number some few very, very much beloved among those I have known for many years.

Charles is delivering a course of lectures at Coventry just now; else were he not absent from home, he would, I know, desire me to add his warm thanks and kind regards to you for all your goodness to his little woman.

FEB. 28TH. I would not post this letter yesterday because I had a sort of half conviction that this morning's post would bring me one from you. It was just one of those vague hopes that schoolchildren indulge, when they affect to disbelieve a matter they wish, in a superstitious fancy that this is the way to bring it about. So I have gone about saying to myself, " I don't expect to hear from my Enthusiast to-morrow." " I know to-morrow's post will bring no pleasant communication from my Enthusiast," etc. But I shall go on trying the charm, and if I don't succeed, I shall reverse the spell, and say, " I am sure another week won't elapse without bringing me the pleasant sight of his handwriting."

The Crystal Palace looks to me finished, but there is still loud noise of workmen there; and I hear they are all mighty busy with the exhibition arrangements in the interior already. Alfred will have a specimen of his music-type printing there.

The Park on a Sunday is crowded, and numberless foreigners are even now arrived in London. Such a hermit-life do I lead that I have not an iota of news to send you. And I hope it is now none to you that I am

Yours very sincerely,
MARY COWDEN CLARKE.

MAR. 18, 1851,
CRAVEN HILL COTTAGE, BAYSWATER.
DEAR ENTHUSIAST:

I MAKE no apology for the egoism of sending you a printed proposal which I circulated once upon a time, touching a monument

[45]

to Shakespeare. I must tell you a good thing of
that wicked Douglas Jerrold's when I showed
him the proposal in the MS. He approved, and
then added: "But you must n't limit the subscription to women only. Remember he was n't
Mrs. Shakespeare." Is n't it like the dear rogue?
I suppose I need n't tell you that the account, in
Coutts's books, remains to this day a blank page!

Why did you conclude your letter with that
expostulatory sentence about a certain intended
dedication? I was reading your letter aloud to
my brother, and he said: "Does n't your Enthusiast know that when a woman holds her tongue
and says nothing in answer to a man who remonstrates with her, that that's a sign she
means to have her own way?" Why, the tale
to be dedicated to you follows immediately after
the one to be dedicated to our honoured Jerrold,
the "Royal Douglas" as you call him. Can you
resist this? It comforts me to find you immediately after, signing yourself "A weak but
warm-hearted old man!" My especial darlings
of humanity are those who are weak from warm-
heartedness — persuadable, coaxable, charming
beings! none of your firm, high-principled
people, as they call themselves — obstinate, odious, inflexible stoics, as others — especially
women — call them!

I am sorry to say, I forget now with which head of Shakespeare I sealed my last to you, or rather, the letter you allude to. You say a "front face." Charles has a ring with a front face, which I had cut out at Mabley's in Wellington Street for him. Mine is a profile; the ring given to me by my brother, on the completion of the Concordance.

When Charles was a young fellow, with more money in his pocket then to idle away in pleasant whims, he too spent a good deal in that tempting shop in Leicester Fields. It was a tempting, fascinating place. I remember, as a child, going with my mother there; and she, with her usual judicious way of giving her children an opportunity of cultivating a taste for the Beautiful in Art as well as Nature, put me on one of the high chairs against the counter, that I might kneel there and peer into the glass cases full of lovely gems. I have a strong impression of the pleasures I then had, as if it were yesterday. Mothers can scarcely calculate the amount of future happiness they may be bestowing, in one such judicious moment of providing their little ones with food for thought and taste.

Indeed, I hardly know anything that would afford me greater delight than the gift you propose of some of those plaster casts. Charles and

I would revel in them. To show you how we love to surround ourselves with attainable classicalities, I 'll tell you how our own snuggery — our own room, part sleeping-room, part scribbling-room — is behung. Over the chimney-piece there are two bas-reliefs, a Venus rising from the bath, and one of the brothers of Iphigenia — from the vase. An exquisite painting — the last my beloved brother Edward ever painted — of Christ and Mary in the garden. A miniature of my dear mother, when a girl — copied by my sister Emma. An oil sketch by my brother Edward, of Christ in the Sepulchre, mourned by the Maries. One copied by him from Rubens, of St. Martin dividing his cloak with the beggars. Six by him; subjects from Chaucer's " Canterbury Tales." A water-colour sketch of M. C. C. as Mistress Quickly, by Havell. An oil sketch of a scene in Devonshire. A daguerreotype of my sister Clara. A plaster-cast group of Cupid and Psyche, and the piping Faun. Over the doorway John of Bologna's Venus; next to her the head of Mercury, with Leigh Hunt's tasteful suggestion of the wings added to the cap. A little lithograph of Westmacott's lovely " Bluebell." Over the bed's head come a copy of Titian's Bacchus and Ariadne, exquisitely executed in miniature by my dear Edward.

An engraving of a subject by Newton from the "Vicar of Wakefield." Two water-colour drawings by Copley Fields. A pencil head of Jean Paul, copied by Emma. A pencil portrait of sister Clara. Portrait of Charles Dickens, engraved, after Maclise. Also of Douglas Jerrold, engraved after daguerreotype. A water-colour copy by Emma, of a favourite of Charles's, a female Satyr, from one of Nicholas Poussin's pictures. A head of a girl, engraved, called "Innocence," one of Charles's loves. Pencil portrait of M. C. C. by dear Edward. Lithograph portrait of Charles's schoolfellow, honoured John Keats. A plaster cast of the Venus de' Medici, and one of the young Apollo. Along the wall on which our eyes open, the first thing every morning, is an engraving of Guido's enchanting "Aurora," and Stothard's Canterbury Pilgrimage, flanked by a bust of our Idol, and one of Milton on the Michael Angelo brackets. The fine face of Shakespeare, engraved. A pencil portrait of Leigh Hunt, by Wageman. An engraving of our friend Humphreys, after Sir Joshua. An oil sketch of a Bacchante and Cupid, by dear Edward. An engraving by Scriven, of Chaucer. A fine engraving of Leslie's "Sancho and the Duchess." A lithograph portrait of my sister Isabella. On the cabinet stands John of

Bologna's charming " Mercury " — all but flying.
Near to him an engraving of Leslie's " Griselda."
And over the doorway leading into the dining-
room a plaster cast of a recumbent Bacchante.

I have thus, my dear sir, given you a notion
of our environments, knowing (judging by myself)
that you will like to be able to form as clear a picture as possible of the room where we usually sit.
I remember it considerably alleviated the pain of
my separation from my dear mother, after I had
been to Nice and knew every detail of her new
home, so that whenever my thoughts flew to her,
they could depict her as she daily was surrounded.
Though we are so near town, yet we have the
delight of a bit of garden-ground. I have told
you that the cottage of the Trihominate is one
of the primeval dwellings left hereabouts. So I
look out, from the table where I write, on to a
grass-plat, some pear and apple trees, and an elm
or two, with laburnum and lilacs. There are a
pair of blackbirds, a thrush, and a robin now on
the grass hopping about. You must know that
Charles has had a shelving bath made for the
birds, which, with plenty of crumbs, brings them
about us in flocks. Pretty creatures ! The thrush
and the blackbirds have already begun to sing,
and we hear them every morning now, with the
first peep of dawn.

If you talk of your being crazy for writing me such a long letter, what will you call me? But it's terribly alluring, this gossiping across the Atlantic; it makes one forget one's duties. Here ought I to have been writing away this morning, and here am I chatting and scribbling with an Enthusiast, who turns one's head with his kind flatteries and makes one forget all duties of industry, etc.

I did not even see that joke you speak of in "Punch" about Mrs. L. and the Duke of Wellington, so I cannot tell you anything about its truth. Poor Mrs. L. is gone to Italy with her daughter, in search of health. They visited Nice, but found it dull, and went on South immediately. The "Song on May Morning" is, I believe, in all the editions of Milton. You know it, surely. You will say so when you see it:

> "Now the bright morning-star, Day's harbinger,
> Comes dancing from the East, and leads with her
> The flowery May, who from her green lap throws
> The yellow cowslip and the pale primrose.
>   Hail, bounteous May that dost inspire
>   Mirth, and youth, and warm desire!
>   Woods and groves are of thy dressing;
>   Hill and dale doth boast thy blessing.
> Thus we salute thee with our early song,
> And welcome thee, and wish thee long."

"Of course! To be sure!" I hear you exclaim.

I dote upon your song of the Katydid. It is
excellent. I am not acquainted with Miss Martineau, but admire her " Deerbrook " and her
" Life in a Sick-room " very much. I have no
doubt she will be very much delighted with your
song and chorus.

MAR. 20. Do you happen to have seen a
cast of The Face from the Stratford-upon-Avon
Monument by a man of the name of Will
Warner? Perhaps you have one. Let me know
this. It is exquisite. We have a copy in the
parlour, that Will Warner himself brought here.
He is a native of Stratford; quite an original;
but a good enthusiastic fellow, as far as I have
seen of him. What a glorious Face and Head it
is! We have a composition monumental bust in
the garden, among the trees, opposite the parlour
windows; and in the hall, the exact copy of the
Monument itself, executed by Mabley, which he
sent to me. I hope you like that portrait pre-
fixed to Collier's fine edition. It has all the
intellect in the upper part of the face, with all
the sweetness and sensibility in the mouth, which
I fancy must be genuinely like. How that face
must have looked when it was penning some
certain passages we wot of! Can't you picture
it to yourself as it must have looked when writing Lear's curse, and then think of it as it must

have smiled when writing some of Falstaff's jests, Touchstone's quips, or Dogberry's humour?

MAR. 21. Excuse great haste in closing this. God bless you, dear sir! and pray believe me

Yours faithfully,

M. C. C.

MAR. 26, 1851,
CRAVEN HILL COTTAGE, BAYSWATER.

DEAR ENTHUSIAST:

I HAVE just written—on the preceding sheet of note paper to this — to Mr. Jerrold, to thank him for a copy of "Punch" (an advance copy, Mar. 29) which he sent me this morning by post, directed in his own hand. You must know, I always kiss that handwriting when I see it. . . .

MAR. 28. Last week I had the pleasure of sending you a letter of chat, which I hope you duly received. How pleasantly sure we feel now in sending a letter to a friend! All owing to that blessed post!

I suppose you will have seen, by the time this reaches you, that Mr. Oxenford has been giving an English version of Molière's fine comedy of "Tartuffe;" in his hands we know how admirably it will be done. I am such a hermit now that I never go to the theatre; but the first night of "Tartuffe" at the Haymarket was a great temptation. However, I was prudent, and

[53]

did not venture into the hot theatre and the night air. I often say that there are only two things now that would take me inside a theatre —a new play, by either Leigh Hunt or Douglas Jerrold. Yes, perhaps, Rachel's acting. Do you know her acting? It is the finest tragedy since the elder Kean's time; and in some things she reminded me much of him, the gestures of her hand especially. In both of those tragedians there was a poetry of suggestion, that I think I never saw in any other acting in equal degree.

I am absolutely without news to tell you, so at once conclude with the non-news that I am, dear friend, Yours faithfully,

MARY COWDEN CLARKE.

Kindest compliments to Mrs. Balmanno and the wicked lord deputy.

———

APRIL 2, 1851,
CRAVEN HILL COTTAGE, BAYSWATER.
DEAR FRIEND:

MANY thanks for a kind letter dated Mar. 19, enclosing one from Mrs. Balmanno, and one for Mr. Mason, which latter of course was posted forthwith. Pray thank Mrs. Balmanno very cordially and sincerely for her kind praise. It is no slight source of self-congratulation to find that the Tales have favour with a

[54]

mind of such elegance and refinement as hers evidently is. In these "fast" times as they are called, when sentiment and generous feeling and artistic taste are voted slow, it is a privilege to find readers who have sympathy with such things as profess to be but "silly sooth," and to "dally with the innocence of love, like the old age."[1]

You have once or twice in your letters, dear sir, hinted at the non-enthusiasm of the two worthier members of the Trihominate, and suppose that they have not a sufficiently high estimation of your "Idol." Now pray, let me disabuse you of so unjust a suspicion. They only too generously rate the worth of their "little woman," as she's sometimes called. They treat her with a sensible, rational candour ; they give her feelings and opinions no less weight than their own, and yet with all the frankness and plain-dealing they would use to a man — the very usage in short, which a woman in the relation I bear to them would wish to receive at a husband's and brother's hands. As to dear old Alf, he and I, when we were mites of children, shared pocket-money, books, toys,

---

[1] ". . . It is silly sooth,
And dallies with the innocence of love,
Like the old age."
— "Twelfth Night," Act II, Scene IV.

all our possessions, in common. We were what we called partners, and we used to agree that when we grew up I should keep his house for him, and that we would never marry. Fate has so happily managed that I actually do that for him, even though a wife, and am his housekeeper as well as my husband's. For twenty-one years after my marriage we all lived together in my father and mother's house ; but when our parents went abroad for the benefit of my mother's health, and the other members of the family had dispersed, we three formed ourselves into the Trihominate, remaining in the cottage. There are not wanting those who will tell you that, notwithstanding her inferiority to the others, M. C. C. is Alf's favourite sister ; but he is so good a brother to all his sisters that it would be difficult to decide which was his favourite. With regard to the other member of the Trihominate, I tell you all when I tell you that Charles and his Molly have long been noted among their intimates for being married lovers. In short, my dear sir, they are only too fond and indulgent; but to tell you the truth, I can't find it in my heart to wish that they should abate one jot of their indulgence. I consent to think less well of their judgment, while I owe so much to their favour.

Now, to endeavour to give you some idea of their persons, in reply to what you inquire about them. Charles is tall, — I'm "just as high as his heart," as Orlando says of his mistress, — fresh-complexioned, of a joyous and enjoying spirit that has won him many fast friends, and he is a universal favourite with the young girls of our acquaintance — an excellent test, you will allow, of a man's winning qualities. Alf is almost the absolute reverse of the picture you have painted of him. He is of middle stature, a regular burly Englishman — brown hair and eyes, a good-humoured mouth, and with a delicious bass voice; which I hope you'll hear some day, if ever that pleasant possibility should ripen into a reality, which you think may bring you to England. . . .

Kneeling is due but to that "Incomprehensible Power" of whom you speak. Let me send you a specimen of homage to that Power, which I would tell you appears to me a fine and pure piece of homage, were I not one in heart and soul with its writer:

HYMN TO GOD

In thy large temple, the blue depth of space,
 And on the altar of thy quiet fields, —
Fit shrine to hold the beauty of thy love, —
 Great Spirit! with earnest cheerfulness I place

This off'ring, which a grateful heart now yields.
  For all those high and gracious thoughts that rove
O'er all thy works; for all the rare delights
  Of eye and ear, — harmonious forms and strains
Of deepest breath; for this ensuing spring,
  With all its tender leaves and blossoming,
And dainty smells that steam from dropping;
  For sunny days and silent shining nights;
For youth, and mirth, and health, tho' dash'd with smarts,
  As luscious creams are tinged with bitterness;
For hope, — sweet hope! unconscious of alloy;
  For peaceful thoughts, kind faces, loving hearts,
That suck out all the poison from distress —
  For all these gifts I offer gratitude and joy!

C. C. C. 1825.

As I am indulging in the conjugo-egoism of sending you C. C. C.'s verses, let me send you a sonnet which I think will prove to you what I endeavoured to impress on you respecting his enthusiasm:

TO MY OWN MARY

I feel my spirit humbled when you call
My love of Home a virtue; 't is the part
Yourself have played has fix'd me; for the heart
Will anchor where its treasure is; and small
As is the love I bear you, 't is my all —
The widow's mite, compar'd with your desert.
You and our quiet room there are the mart
Of all my thoughts; 't is there they rise and fall.

The parent bird that in its wanderings
O'er hill and dale, thro' copse and leafy spray,
Sees naught to lure his constant heart away
From her who gravely sits with furled wings,
Watching their mutual charge — howe'er he roam,
His eye still fixes on his mossy home.

C. C. C. Oct. 14, 1832.

[58]

APRIL 4, 1851.

Charles encloses the lock of hair[1] you desire, with many thanks for the feeling which inspired the wish to possess it. But he particularly requests that you will not think of carrying out your proposal to share the other venerated lock you speak of. It will be in far better hands where it is at present. To tell you the truth, my dear sir, — I hope you won't think ill of us for it! — we are but sorry relic-preservers. Nor have we ever been collectors of Autographs. I trust you will not despise us for such a piece of bad taste; but so it is. And I feel it right candidly to confess to you our defect in that matter; as, after all, we sink ourselves less in the estimation of a true friend, by a sincere confession of error, than by an affectation of an unpossessed taste.

Pray, my dear sir, do not be so anxious about possible repetitions. Persons who write constantly and fully to each other must needs occasionally repeat news or subjects. My dear mother and I, who are almost journal-like in our

---

[1] This lock of hair is dark brown. It lay carefully folded in a paper within this letter, marked, "Lock of Mary Cowden Clarke's hair sent me by her husband, at my request.

"ROBERT BALMANNO."

letters, make a rule to care no jot whether we repeat or not. Besides, in being too anxious lest you should send a repetition of a formerly told story, you may, by leaving it out, deprive me of a very pleasant relation. Be not careful, then, as to whether you repeat or no; suffice it that your letters are extremely pleasant and entertaining.

I am sure that I ought to make apologies, if apologies are at all needful, for the egotistical detail with which my letters to you abound; but you have made me so perpetually feel that your " darling " is the most interesting subject I can choose for you that it is partly your own fault, my dear sir. Like Tony Lumpkin's speech to his mother, I may say: " Ecod, you 've spoiled me, so you must e'en take me for your pains!" With this pleasant reflection, I take my leave for the present, and subscribe myself, dear friend,

Your grateful

M. C. C.

APRIL 23RD, 1851,
CRAVEN HILL COTTAGE, BAYSWATER.

DEAR ENTHUSIAST:

I HAVE to thank you for two charming letters of March 26 and April 8. Let me hasten to relieve you of the principal source of anxiety in the last. It would be wrong to doubt the sincerity of the repugnance you express to have one of these stories dedicated to you; yet allow me to say, I think your modesty in declining it excessive. Why should you allege the being "a poor clerk in a public office" as a reason against receiving the sincere homage of a friend? "A man's a man for a' that"— very often a better man "for that," inasmuch as he chooses to earn his own bread instead of being obliged for it to other people. . . . Surely rank has nothing to do with "insignificance," "worthlessness"— as you plead for reasons; "The man of independent mind he looks and laughs at a' that."

> "A prince can make a belted knight
> A marquis, duke and a' that;
> But an honest man 's aboon his might,
> Guid faith he maunna fa' that.
> For a' that, and a' that,
> Their dignities, and a' that,
> The pith o' sense, and pride o' worth,
> Are higher rank than a' that."

At the same time, I feel that I have no right to press the matter. I can readily understand that a feeling of modesty such as this may appear very differently to another than it does to the person who entertains it. I will only thus far presume on the privilege we women have of persevering on a point where we have set our hearts

— I will ask you whether you would have any
objection to the dedication thus worded: "To
her known and unknown friend 'The American
Enthusiast' this tale is gratefully dedicated by
Mary Cowden Clarke." Now, my dear sir, this
will respect your scruples of modesty by not
suffering your name to appear, at the same time
that it will gratify my wish of inscribing one of
the tales to the kind friend who has given me so
large a share of his heart and won so large a
share of mine. He and I will know the secret,
while to the world it will be suffered to remain
a mystery, perhaps somewhat piquant and interesting. What say you? But still, if you have
the least objection remaining, tell me so frankly,
and the dedication shall even thus be cancelled;
there will be still time, if you write to me by return of post.

You will perceive by the date of this letter
that I received your last on the eve of the day
you are proposing to celebrate in a proper spirit
of hilarity; so that I am able to think of you
during your birthday delights, which is very
pleasant. I am up at six, writing opposite to
the windows you wot of; the April freshness is
on leaf and grass, and there is a merry rogue of
a throstle, whistling up in the elms "with his note
so true." Charles is sitting beside me at the

Charles Cowden Clarke

same table, writing away at his new course for
the London Institution. I will send you the
syllabus that you may see that he is occupied
with the appropriate subject for the day. It was
almost sacrilege to quote any other poet than
Himself this morning; but dear true-hearted
Burns has a right, if any one has, to be quoted
and revelled in on Shakespeare's day.

I have to thank you, dear friend, for the vignette — a copy in each letter. It is extremely
tasteful; and were it not so much more consonant with the Enthusiast's feelings than consistent
with the merits of the little woman therein honoured, I should say it is very charming. Now,
however, each time I look at it, I am obliged to
remind myself of the warmth and kindness of the
enthusiasm that prompted it, in order to coun-
teract the sense of humiliation with which it inspires me. Over-honouring, so far from inspiring
pride, rather inspires mortification, rousing the
consciousness of shortcomings and unworthiness,
in lieu of such imputed excellence. With regard
to resemblance, Alfred, especially, thinks it like ;
and with a courtesy of allowance, it is probably
very like what I was when I first began my
labour of love. I was then just twenty. As the
man says in one of Knowles's plays, "Thou
hast worked with thy pencil and slate, Master

Thomas," [1] and therefore you can tell how many
years have elapsed since the one in which I told
you I wrote the first line of the Concordance!
You made me smile by what you said about the
eyelash. Why, my dear sir, all young ladies give
their portraits good eyelashes; and Emma is no
exception to the rule of young lady artists. Between her and your artist, M. C. C.'s profile has
been softened down and improved, until it is so
comely that I can only wish, etc. I flatter myself I am half as good-looking. But "something
too much of this." Charles bid me thank you
very cordially for the copies you are so kind as
to promise him; and the Trihominate all join in
acknowledging the kind spirit which prompted
the execution of the vignette, and the honour it
is intended to do them. I had already antici-
pated what would probably be your answer with
regard to the Face, and I do not fancy poor Will
Warner has been so good a manager as to get
his work yet known across the Atlantic; in this
anticipation, therefore, I had already written to
Warner desiring him to send me the casts.
They are arrived. One I mean for Nice; the
other I hope my dear Enthusiast will do me
the favour to accept from his "darling," in remembrance of her and of our joint Idol, whom

---

[1] "The Hunchback." Sheridan Knowles.

it presents so faithfully. There is even the inequality of the muscles of the face on either cheek, which Warner so graciously pointed out to me as marking the probability of the monumental face having been taken from the life after death. (A Hibernianism! but forgive it.) What a divine face it is! It is a fitting external interpretation of the brain that informed it. " How noble in reason! how infinite in faculty! . . . in apprehension how like a god! "[1]

I have written down to Whittaker's to endeavour to obtain a copy of the print affixed to Collier's edition, my favourite portrait of him. It hangs close to my bedside. It is one of those portraits that look at you, and I have a strange fancy for turning toward it whenever anything vexes or perplexes my spirit; the expression of those bland, benignant eyes full of intelligence, and that mouth, full of sweetness and sensibility, seem to have a supernatural power of reaching and sympathizing with poor humanity and consoling its struggles, with their divine influence. I shall hope to obtain the copy in time to enclose it in the case with the Face, which I trust will leave England this week. It will be delightful to me to think of your looking upon these two effigies of our Idol and sharing with me some of

[1] " Hamlet," Act II, Scene II.

the delightful thoughts with which they have
supplied me.

No, dear sir, I do not at all think it "passing
strange" that you should choose to be "in perfect
cue" when you sit down to the reading of certain
Tales that you honour with your approbation.
I can too entirely sympathize with such whims
of feeling to find them strange. I like to be in
a happy mood, a meek state of soul, a fit frame
of being, when I sit down to the perusal of certain writings I like. I can't bear to be disturbed;
I like to yield myself up to all the emotions and
abstracted fancies that such writings engender.
I quite agree with Charles Lamb in his essay
on " Grace Before Meat." Why have we none
for books, those spiritual repasts? and grace
before Milton? a grace before Shakespeare? a
devotional exercise proper to be said before reading the " Faerie Queene"? One likes to be
choice in the seasons as well as the selection of
books. Charles and I have but slender time for
reading. What do you think we do? There is
a certain one-quarter of an hour or twenty minutes after breakfast when we wait for Alf, who is
apt to come down later than we do, and during
that period Charles reads to me some dainty
morsel. Just now we have a bit of Bacon for
breakfast — Verulam Bacon, I mean. We are on

a course of that fine relishing old fellow, and racy and savoury and pungent and exquisitely choice do we find him upon reperusal. We once went through all the "Paradise Lost" in the same way. At another time, Wordsworth's "Excursion," and his lovely Sonnets. A mere taste such as this, daily, of such fine matter, sends one through the day with a well-attuned spirit to meet what the work-a-day world hath in store.

I knew you would be pleased to have the description of the place your "darling" inhabits; it is so pleasant to picture the precise environments of those we love.

With the kindest remembrances of the Trihominate to Mrs. B. and yourself, not forgetting "the Wicked Lord Deputy," pray believe me to be

Yours affectionately,

M. C. C.

MAY DAY, 1851,
CRAVEN HILL COTTAGE, BAYSWATER.
MY DEAR ENTHUSIAST:

ALL the world are gone to the opening of the Exhibition, of course, but here is your "darling" playing Cinderella, having given her Abigail leave to go and see the show. This little nest looks as quiet to-day as though it

[67]

were not within a stone's throw of Hyde Park,
where all the globe's people are congregating to
meet the Queen of England. I hear it is to be
a very grand affair, indeed — the state carriage
and cream horses, a procession almost like a
coronation day. I have just seen Alf off, — and
some home-made gingerbread, lest he should
starve, shut up in the Crystal Palace for all these
hours. He, as one of the choir of Lincoln's Inn
Company, of Bencher's chapel, sings in the Royal
music that is to greet Her Majesty there. Fortunately, it is lovely weather, a bright morning.
I trust it may not turn out showery, for the
honour of old England, lest the foreigners have
a laugh extra at our climate.

And now to reply to your last kind letter, dear
sir. I read it in the Park, through which I walk
each morning with my dear men-folks, on their
way to business. It was very delightful to my
feelings, as you may suppose, to think of such
an honour paid me so far away West! To be
toasted in champagne bumpers by a reverend
gentleman and his three "womankind" is indeed
a proud privilege. There is something exquisitely flattering in the thought of having inspired
such a piece of vivacity in such beings. Pray,
tell the Rev. Mr. Tracy, when next you write to
him, that his kind compliment made my heart

dance for joy, and if I had not been out in Hyde
Park I might have literally committed the vagary
of dancing for joy. As it was, the being in the
open air, while such glad feelings possessed me,
had the effect of giving me the notion that some
of the pleasurable emotion caused by his and your
kindness, by sympathy travelled back to those
who originated it. I wonder whether you or the
Rev. Mr. Tracy, about ten o'clock on that particular morning, were conscious of any sympathetic
impression that caused you to feel more than
ordinarily jocund? My mother has strong notions on the subject of sympathies of this kind, and
her eldest daughter inherits somewhat of her
creed. I don't know whether I told you that
your kind doctor — Dr. Storrar of Helena, you
know — desired me, as I valued my health, to
walk daily, so I accompany my men-folks of a
morning on their way to town, as far as the Marble
Arch — old Cumberland gate, you remember.
The post generally comes in before they leave
home, and we read our letters to each other as
we walk through the Park; so I often enjoy
those of my dear Enthusiast in the open air
— a double delight!

This being May morning, Charles has just
repeated to me Milton's lovely song; he is now
gone to Dean Street, and I have sat down to

chat with my kind Enthusiast. Let me wish him and his dear Mary joy, on this the anniversary of their wedding day. My dear Richardson makes his heroine say that the anniversary of the wedding day is a happier day to a woman than the day itself, and I cordially agree with him.

Who should come in, quite unexpectedly, the other morning, but Emma? The Miss Rolls were impatient to return to England, and so they left Naples, and came home unannounced. The Neapolitan Government are curiously paternal in their postal arrangements, choosing what letters their children shall receive. So it unfortunately happened that Emma never received my last letter to her there, stating your wishes with respect to the Vatican inquiries at Rome. I have hardly seen her yet; so that I have had no time for a quiet chat with her, to tell her all about the honour you have done her sketch. She will, I know, be perfectly astounded, for she has a most depreciating notion of all she does. To find, therefore, that a little sketch she made idly one evening, while Charles was reading and I working, merely to employ her pencil, has been made so much of, all across the ocean, will be an incomprehensible marvel.

I beg your pardon, my dear sir, Dowton was *not* before my time. I remember him well, as if it were but yesterday. Dear Miss Lamb[1] told me once, as a child, to take great care in remembering actors that I then saw; as, if I lived to be an old woman, it would be pleasant to tell of them to those younger than myself. I remember she told me this on the occasion of my being taken to see Munden, on one of his last performances. He played Old Dornton,[2] and Crack the cobbler, that night. In consequence of beloved and wise Mary Lamb's hint, I have him as well fixed in my mind's eye as though he had been seen by me last week. I fancy I see him now, as, in the latter character, he hovered round the table where stood the brown jug, saying, "Some gentleman has left his ale," and, after an ineffable glance at the audience, adding, "and some other gentleman 'll drink it!" I can recall the exact intonation in which many of the words were uttered by some of the great actors I then saw and heard. So valuable is such a hint from such a woman to a young girl. Can I ever forget the subdued, oily tones of Dowton as Cantwell,[3] calling to his nephew "Charles!" in an early scene of the play; and afterwards his haughty, imperious, violent voice, when he

---

[1] Mrs. Clarke was Mary Lamb's namesake.
[2] "Road to Ruin." Holcroft.
[3] Dr. Cantwell, in "The Hypocrite," by Bickerstaff.

shouted to him; or the tremendous depth of concentrated malice and defeated will with which he uttered that one word "D—n," in the same play?

I envy you your remembrance of the glorious Mrs. Siddons and the enchanting Mrs. Jordan. I have heard my father speak of Mrs. Jordan's laugh, and from the way in which he spoke of her I have always fancied she was one of his boyish flames. It must be a great treat to witness your imitation of Cooke's Sir Pertinax.[1] I once saw Young in the character. He was very good, but, I have heard, greatly inferior to Cooke in the same part. I always liked Young's comedy better than his tragedy, with the exception of his Iago, which was fine. But for tragedy, what could equal Kean's Othello? It shakes me even now, to think of his mode of uttering, "Not a jot, not a jot!" And the whole of that grand third scene of the third act was one of the most awful representations of a passion-stirred man that can be conceived. Some of the inflections of Kean's voice were unsurpassed for their power of moving the soul, to my thinking. Do you remember his scene with Tubal, in Shylock? And those two terrible

---

[1] Sir Pertinax MacSycophant, in "The Man of the World," by Macklin.

sounds in the dying scene of his Sir Giles
Overreach? They make me tremble, only to
think of them. At the time, I recollect, they
made me almost ill with awe. I have bethought
me that I have made some mistake in believing
the first of May to be your wedding day. I
remember, in one of your letters, your telling
me that since your marriage you and your Mary
make holiday on that day annually; and so
I probably fancied it to be your wedding day
from that circumstance. I lately inquired, too,
whether Angelo were your only child, and since
then I have recollected that in one of your
letters you speak of your two boys. What is
the other one's name? . . .

There is something very pretty and attractive
in the name of Brooklyn. Is it a suburb of New
York, or how? Tell me a little about it. I can
fancy your passing your evenings very pleasantly
with so accomplished a wife, with your two sons,
and with your literary and artistic tastes. I find
you are in the habit of writing late at night; does
it not try your eyes? It often amazes me to find
that you can write that small and exquisitely cut
handwriting by candle light. My sight won't let
me write at night, and I am some years younger.
I was born in 1809, so that I am more than
"fat, fair, and forty;" though not much of the

first, and still less of the second. I was going
to say that I heard you say (but I have *seen* you
say) that you have reached seventy; now it is
a glorious privilege to be able to write such
a beautiful legible hand as yours, by candle
light, after having looked upon the world for so
many years. Have you any secret for preserving
such an eagle sight? If so, pray impart it to
me. I have sometimes pictured to myself your
face. I believe I have come to no very precise
linear notions about it, but I have a general impression that it must be something like that
venerable friend's of Jean Paul Richter, who
says of it: "In his seventy-second year his face
is a thanksgiving for his former life, and a love-
letter to all mankind." I can imagine your
voice, — I am a lover of pleasant-speaking voices,
— and I fancy it clear, ringing, full of hilarity and
full of cordial sympathy; I can imagine it saying the very kindest things in a playful tone. I
wish Mrs. Balmanno would tell me what it is
like. I have a notion you have somewhat
roguish eyes — like Elliston's; I forbear to
question Mrs. Balmanno on this point. Charles
tells me he remembers your face perfectly; and
says you are tall.

The young blackbirds are flown. It is very
pretty to see the parent birds flying to and fro

and hopping about the grass plat, busily collecting food for the little ones, who flutter clumsily
about among the low twigs and sit hunching
all of a heap in the hedge, waiting to be fed.
It is very pleasant to have them so tame about
us. Our garden is almost the only spot left of
the aboriginal enclosures that used to be so rife
at Bayswater.

I fancy the house you mention at Westbourne
Green as having belonged to Mrs. Siddons is
no longer in existence. Hosts of new villas
have sprung up in that neighbourhood, displac-
ing the pleasant old-fashioned suburban homes.
The Great Western Railroad crosses the neighbourhood; the ground has been raised to a
higher level all around; and that beautiful mansion and ground which you probably remember
near there as having belonged to some nobleman was converted into railway offices, I believe. They have been pulling down the old
wall that skirted Kensington Gardens along the
Bayswater Road, replacing it by an iron railing.
This will be an improvement, affording a view
into that charming place; and we hope they
will give us a gate not far from the end of our
lane, so that we shall be able to walk to town
through a part of the gardens as well as through
the Park.

A friend has sent Alfred some lovely plants of geraniums and cinerarias; like a kind brother, as he is, he has brought up two of the former and put them on my writing table, knowing how I love flowers. I enclose one of the exquisite petals, though I fear it will not retain its colour. . . .

With Trihominate kindest greetings, believe me to be, dear friend,

Yours gratefully,

MARY COWDEN CLARKE.

½ P. 3 A.M., MAY 27, 1851,
CRAVEN HILL COTTAGE, BAYSWATER.

DEAR ENTHUSIAST:

YOUR letter of the 13th arrived yesterday, bringing me the unwelcome news of your having been so seriously ill. I cannot sleep for thinking about you, and so get up to chat with you on paper by this charming soft morning light. The sky looks so clear and cloudless, and all is so exquisitely still, that it seems as though the spirits of friends could have freer communion, writing to each other at such a time. It is a great comfort to know that you are better. I know how terribly weak and depressed that fearful influenza leaves the frame;

so that I trust the sad tone of your letter arises
principally from that cause, and that your next
may bring me word of your entire recovery.
You may readily imagine how it touched and
delighted me to find that my letters afforded
you satisfaction during your illness. It is indeed
a privilege to be allowed thus to minister to a
friend's comfort at the time he most needs
sympathy and solace.

I have to acknowledge, dear sir, a most
charming letter of yours dated April 27th, a
note to Charles, of the 23d, and a packet from
Delf's containing the engravings you so obligingly sent us. The portraits are very pretty;
but between ourselves they can scarcely be
called *illustrations*, at least of the girlhood
heroines. Helena and Isabella, by their very
dresses, are the Helena and Isabella of the plays,
not of the Tales. The latter picture might,
I think, have been called "Sister Aloyica"
better; but as Mr. Toots says, "It's of no consequence, thank you!" I think the "Venice"
particularly good, both in itself and as an illustration. Many, many thanks for your kindness
in sending them to me, and for the American
copies of the stories; it is a proud and pleasant
thing to see one's self in Transatlantic print!

I have been very closely at work lately; so

much so that I have not yet been to the Exhibition. Indeed, I have been out nowhere. Yes, I've had three especial treats this season; one was the dress rehearsal at Devonshire House, and to which my beloved manager invited in his own kind way. I had the gratification of seeing several venerated faces among the audience, as well as on the stage—honoured literary and artistic heads. Leigh Hunt was there, and a seat happening to become vacant by my side, he did me the honour of coming and occupying it of his own accord, with one of his own graceful and gracious speeches. I had thus an opportunity of mentioning you to him; he bade me tell you of his cordial remembrance, when next I should write to you. To Miss Kelly also I had an opportunity of speaking in the drawing-room, where the company assembled previous to the performance. I told her of an enthusiastic admirer of hers, who spoke of her as "darling little Kelly," for that she lived thus in his recollection. It was pleasant to see the face—faded from the youth and energy it once had, but with the intelligential beauty that years cannot destroy—looking pleased and beaming to hear of this. There were two other treats: one the first performance of Douglas Jerrold's new comedy, "Retired from Business"

[78]

—for which he kindly sent us tickets; and the other my sitting beside him at a dinner party soon after. That is one of the few pleasures of an English dinner party; if you do happen to sit next to a pleasant person, you can enjoy a very snug chat. How passing delightful then, when you happen to be placed near to one of your idols. I am a bit of an idolater, you know!

Talking of idols — there is one of mine in town now, who indulged us last Sunday evening with several hours of her magic potency. She is a German lady, who has Beethoven at her fingers' ends, and better still, in her soul. She has a prodigious memory, and can play a whole library of his enchanting sonatas by heart. I think I never heard her play more divinely than she did last Sunday. I was rapt into the seventh Heaven. Such music so played puts one's heart and mind into a happy mood for hours, nay, for days afterwards. The sun has risen, and there is such a glorious light upon the garden, among the trees and upon the grass. If your dear Mary could behold it, I am sure it would inspire her with something very charming; it is quite a poet's light. It is a great privilege to have such a spot to look out upon from one's bedroom window, living so near to the heart of a great metropolis like London. There is not a day passes but I am grateful that it is so, but alas, they are closing round us with their buildings — their odious "improvements," as they call them. I saw a rope fixed to one of the elms in the field yesterday afternoon; the rest of the dear old trees were marked. I could fancy I heard the Hamadryads moan; I know *I* did.

I cannot express to you, my dear sir, how profoundly I was touched by those passages in your letter of the 27th April where you attribute a happy change in your moral being to the circumstance of our friendship. To make her men friends happier, therefore better, is surely the highest prerogative of woman. It was a subtle compliment, dear friend, and like your kind self to pay it to me. I assure you it made me very happy.

You ask in that letter whether Charles or Alfred wears a moustache. Neither. My Italian brother-in-law Gigliucci wears a long beard, and indeed looks like one of Titian's noblemen stepped out of his frame. He is very handsome, and this fashion suits his style of countenance. My little niece and godchild, Mary Serle, when she first saw the Count, called him " the gentleman with hair on his face."

My mother's address is simply: Madame Novello, Casa Salir, Nice, Sardinia. Nice is as much a French place as an Italian, in the language used. The people speak mostly a wretched patois, compounded from French and Italian. Once when Charles and Alf and I made a peregrination among the mountains in the vicinity there, we fell in with a man in a lonely campagna, who could scarcely make himself understood by us. We could comprehend his native courtesy, through the kindness with which he brought us fresh water from the well, and grapes — such grapes!

I have to thank you for the paper you sent with the announcement respecting Mrs. Forrest.[1] I don't wonder at your receiving hearty testimonials of approval and honour for your giving your support to the cause of an oppressed and injured woman. What an incredible ruffian he seems to be!

Thank you for the manner in which you sanction the dedication as it now stands; it gives me great pleasure. When my mother first learned my plan for the book of Tales, and we discussed it together, she said: "You should dedicate one of them to your friend the American Enthusiast, Victoria." I told her that I had already thought of doing so. We are in the

---

[1] Wife of Edwin Forrest, the actor.

habit of consulting each other in family council in most things we undertake; and it is pleasant to find among people who love each other so dearly, and who have so many ideas in common, and so entirely the same interest at heart, how frequently and strikingly this is proved, by our finding out that we have severally thought of identically the same things previous to consultation. Many thanks for your kind intimation that our young friends, "the girls, dance off merrily!"

And now to reply to your very kind offer of sending me an American bird. I should like one, of all things, especially as your gift, but — you will excuse my being as frank on this point as I have been in all the like cases with you — I own I have an insuperable objection to keeping a bird in a cage. It is this very feeling which makes me take so much delight in the birds in our garden. I can watch them from day to day; nay, they are so tame that they come constantly, and I know them individually. But they are free — they are at liberty; and I have so much of the Englishwoman in me as to make that an essential part of my delight in looking upon them, to know that they are so. Do not be displeased with me, dear sir, for being thus candid with you in response to your kind offer.

Trusting soon to have news that you are quite

well and strong, and with kindest wishes and
regards from the men-folk, believe me to be,
dear friend,

Yours affectionately,

MARY COWDEN CLARKE.

Best compliments and regards to Mrs. Balmanno and the Lord Deputy.

JUNE 18, 1851,
CRAVEN HILL COTTAGE, BAYSWATER.

DEAR ENTHUSIAST:

I AM enchanted to find by your last letter,
dated 23 and 29 of May, that you are recovered from your severe attack of illness.
Pleasant as your letters are throughout, the
most pleasant words in the last were those of
its concluding sentence: "Thank Heaven, I
am at last comparatively well." Charles and I
only yesterday went out for the first time to the
great Exhibition. We are such hermits, and so
very busy, we have not afforded ourselves a day's
holiday for an age, until yesterday and the day
before. On Monday we went with a country
friend, who for years has gone with us, to the
Royal Academy Exhibition.

I like each season to see what Art is doing
among the moderns. There is a droll school of

[83]

young men just started up, who are called, or
who call themselves, the Pre-Raffaellites. You
can hardly conceive of a thing more ludicrous
than their productions. There is one — a picture of "Mariana in the Moated Grange" of
Tennyson by a young artist of the name of Millais. Wonderful! Why take a poetical subject,
and treat it so utterly unpoetically? Mariana,
if such as Mr. Millais represents her, almost jus-
tifies Angelo's desertion! And the worst of it
is that these young men possess undoubted
mechanical skill. There is an effect of lamp-
light in this very picture extremely beautiful;
and the rat on the floor is unexceptionably
painted. But Mariana herself is indulging in a
most portentous yawn — actually stretching herself, or else ascertaining the fit of her dress by
pressing down the waist with both hands behind!
Leslie is charming as usual this year; he is
always successful in his Shakespeare subjects,
and this one is the famous acting-bout between
Falstaff and Hal.

Afterwards, we went to the Exhibition of Old
Masters in Pall Mall, a treat that Charles and I
always give ourselves annually. It is a great
privilege to have the best gems culled from
private collections and presented for public enjoyment once a year. This year there is a cele-

brated "Three Maries" of Annibale Caracci,
belonging to Earl Carlisle. What a terrible
truth there is in this small square of canvas!
The anguish, the passion of woe, in the face of
Mary Magdalene is positively awful. It affected
me so violently that I could hardly trust myself
to look at her countenance; each time I glanced
at it, I fell into fresh agitation. Those grand
old fellows trusted to nature; if they were to
give you a woman in grief, they gave her to you
in all her swollen features, her red eyes, her ugliness of sorrow; but they knew how to redeem
the mere mechanics of their art by the feeling,
the ideality, the sublimity which belongs to passion. You are moved by their touches, as you
are by those of that other masterhand, at once so
simple and so profound. "But yet the pity of
it, Iago! O Iago, the pity of it, Iago!" I will
not enter into the question of the great Exhibition, you will have seen an account of its wonders
in the paper. Suffice that Charles and I were
more than delighted to the degree of our antici-
pations, and that is saying all.

I entirely sympathize with what you say, so
charmingly, about the influence of the open air
upon the feelings and the conscious power of
writing. The worst of it is, that power too often
exhales with the transitory consciousness. Still,

the passing sense of it is delightful. More tall green trees, yesterday in Kensington Gardens; the exquisite underlight, the shadows upon the turf, filled me with delicious emotion; but this morning, so far from being fit for work, I am a wretch, a half-headachy, good-for-nothing, stupid idler, unable to write a line, so sit down to "bestow my tedious of your worship."[1] You see how unceremoniously your indulgence has brought me to treat you.

Charles remembers Irish Johnstone, and "remembers him worthy of thy praise," although I do not. But I do remember Fawcett quite well. I remember his little Isaac in the "Duenna," with dear Mrs. Davenport as the Duenna herself. What a glorious woman that was, — as being very humorous! But one of the best things, to my mind, that I ever saw him play was Sir Francis Wronghead. His way of embarrassedly playing on the ground with the point of his cane when he said, "I doubt I cried 'ay' when I ought to have said 'no,'" was the perfect picture of a bewildered and half-abashed country gentleman.

---

[1] *Dogberry.* If I were as tedious as a king, I could find it in my heart to bestow it all of your worship.
 Leonato. All thy tediousness on me, ah?
 — "Much Ado About Nothing," Act III, Scene V.

I shall especially like to have the map or
sketch of New York you promise me, and the
sketch of your parlours. It will be so very pleasant to see the spot precisely of your daily whereabouts. I am going to be very bold, and to ask
you a favour. Will you make me just such a
candle-shade as you describe? I shall like to
have it in constant use, when we are enjoying
our Trihominate quiet evenings.

Thank you for your personal description of
yourself. I am glad you are bald; I reverence
a bald head. My father is very bald; our Idol
is very bald, *outside* his head! I 'll send you an
engraving we have of my father, after a picture
by my brother. It is allowed, by all who know
Vincent Novello, to be an admirable likeness.
I would with pleasure comply with your wish of
sending you a cutting of that geranium, but I
don't know which it is. Alf sends up to my
room such a succession as not to know which
happened to be the one on my table at the time.
However, I 'll ask him for a cutting of a very
beautiful new sort, which I 've heard him speak
of having had lately. I have not seen Mr. Putnam yet, but shall have much pleasure in meeting him again.

Do you know anything of a book called " The
Scarlet Letter "? It was recommended to me,

by a lady of whose judgment I have a high opinion, the other day. The author, I hear, is an American. His name — which I suspect to be an assumed one — purports to be Nathaniel Hawthorne. That, and a spirited sketch of a Custom House scene and its clerks, associated the work naturally in my mind with you, dear sir. It is by the author of " The House of the Seven Gables." With " The Scarlet Letter " I was extremely interested. There is some powerful feeling, thinking, and writing in it ; and there is great originality in the story and its treatment, though one of the characters reminds me of Henbane, the physician, in Scott's " Fair Maid of Perth;" and another of a human Undine. There are two of the chapters every page of which I think I scored with my pencil as I read on. Pray tell me if you know anything of the writer. Some touches made me think it was written by a woman ; but on the whole I am inclined to think it is a man.

One of the objects of art that most especially charmed us yesterday in the Exhibition was also the creation of an American, I mean the " Greek Slave," — a small marble statue by Mr. Powers. You have, of course, heard of the admiration which, I believe, it has generally excited here. Charles is enthusiastic in his

ÆT. 53
1834

praise; says it is worthy of the antique art. It is exquisitely simple in attitude; very lovely in form, with the expression of the countenance finely illustrative of the subject. It is sorrowful, even resentful, yet not the least sullen; it is full of beauty and even gentle sweetness, yet indignant. We were very much struck with it.

Among the Italian sculpture there is a group of Dante's " Paolo and Francesca." We saw it in the Brera gallery at Milan, which had an exhibition of modern art when we were there in 1847. I little expected ever to have the delight of beholding that group again, especially in England. It is finely poetical. The figures are absolutely floating on the hell-storm. The expression of both faces is admirable, but especially of Paolo's. It is very great. The sculptor's name is Gaetano Motelli; I remember taking it down at the time, for the sake of its delicious Italian euphony, and for the sake of the high excellence of his group. My sister Sabilla sent me over a pen and ink copy she made for an engraving of it, knowing how deeply I fell in love with the original; but I little thought I should have the delight of beholding itself again. Do you know that your birthday is in the same month as my Charles's? Mine is next Sunday, June 27.

FRIDAY, JUNE 20. To-day's post has brought

us our weekly delight in the shape of a "Nice letter." All well, thank God! With kindest remembrances to Mrs. Balmanno, Mr. Angelo, and yourself, believe me to be

Yours faithfully,

MARY COWDEN CLARKE.

Trihominate's regards to the Brooklyn Trio.

JULY 4, 1851,
CRAVEN HILL COTTAGE, BAYSWATER.

DEAR FATHER-IN-LOVE:

SINCE you have invented that pretty title — I have to thank you for a charming long letter dated June 13th, and also for a kind little note by Mr. Putnam, containing two George-the-Third silver pieces and a silvery distich. For each and all, thanks. I honestly remitted Alf's share, and as for the skipping rope, I shall scrupulously invest the money in that article next winter. I have for a long time found an excellent substitute for exercise — in this most changeable climate, when a daily walk is out of the question — in a shower-bath every morning; nothing puts such vigour into both frame and spirit. It is delightful to find you quite restored to your own elastic self; taking a walk of six or

[90]

eight miles without fatigue, and "charming well again." Long may you continue so!

Mr. Putnam did me the favour to call upon me one morning after having been to the Exhibition. It was pleasant to find him so enthusiastic about the beauty of our dear old Kensington Gardens; he seemed quite impressed with the charm of the place. I don't wonder; in itself it is lovely. But immediately after the glare and excitement and giddy wonder of the Crystal Palace, to come through that quiet green place under the fine old trees must have been especially striking. He seems to have much quiet enthusiasm, — a pleasant quality. Alfred afterwards met him at a public meeting, and had the pleasure of some conversation with him. He very politely brought me some of the tales printed by him, and expressed himself very obligingly concerning them. This, among other gratifications, I owe to you, dear sir.

Your account of your "common American mechanic, in a workshop of seventeen pair of stairs" and of what he said, charmed us all as you may imagine, extremely. It is a fine promise for the generation to come, this intellectual reverence and intercommunion. This mechanic's acquaintance with and love for the Warwickshire yeoman's works, and those connected with him, must inevitably be for his happiness and improvement. *Evviva* printing and steam communication! It is curious your mentioning a wood-turner whom you knew so intelligent. In the great Exhibition Charles and I were admiring an exquisite group of wood-carving, next to which stood two common-looking men, and mean in dress. The remarks we overheard them make to each other concerning the workmanship and execution of the carving were so intelligent that Charles joined in their conversation; and I assure you, their mode of expressing themselves and the knowledge of their craft that they discovered would have done honour to a highly educated man, and greatly enhanced our pleasure on all accounts.

How charming the effect was of that little passage in your letter where you describe your having been to look at the glory of the full moon, in the midst of your letter-writing. This blending of the enjoyment of nature with the exercise of the faculties is one of the highest privileges of humanity. It gives a poetical charm to daily existence ; and then the immediate effect of this in the midst of your writing to me — it gave a charming reality and presence to the letter. It is this " writing of the moment " which to me imparts the peculiar fascination of Richardson's style. I am a great admirer of Richardson; I make a point of reading his " Clarissa " and " Sir Charles " alternately, about every other year.

I knew that you would be pleased at my mentioning that I had met Douglas Jerrold. I ought to have told you that the acting of the comedy was admirable; his was excellent. It was a pity he could not have put those intellectual eyes of his into his pocket, for the truer personation of Mr. Softhead. But it was best as it was. His drunken scene was excellent. Still better his after-scene ; where the qualms of his carouse and his remorse haunt him equally. Charles Dickens is a great actor, a fine actor. Were he not pre-eminent as an author, and that we can't spare him in that capacity, it were to be regretted that he is not on the stage. But this too is far best as it is. It was very pleasant, your mention of Mr. Pritchatt and his new-married wife, and that they should have been able to tell our Enthusiast that they had seen us at the London Institution.

You ask me where I usually write. In my own room, the room I described to you so minutely, knowing your enthusiasm would take pleasure in the detail. I am so addle-brained if I have the least distraction when I write, that I shut myself up in my den at that time. That's a byword of

ours you must know, "dennish." My sister Cecilia[1] sometimes comes over to see me, and she
steals upstairs to my room and peeps in and says,
"Are you *dennish?* Or may I come in and have
a chat with you?" You ask me whether I do
not find it a delightful employment to write these
tales. Indeed I do. So intense is my enjoyment of my subject, and so interesting and ex-
citing to me is the endeavour to work it out,
that it gives me a pleasure which I should be
afraid to confess to any one but my Enthusiast.
I hope to finish my twelfth story to-day. I have
just about another day's work to do to it, so I
am up at this early hour, half-past four, and have
had my shower bath, that I may not trench upon
the time I devote to it, by writing this letter then.
By this management I get two pleasures into
the day.

I don't know the Vandyke portrait you mention, the Gonsalvi.[2] In what collection is it?
Dear Dulwich, where the other portrait you
mention — Sir Joshua's Mrs. Siddons — is enshrined! What an exquisite place is that Dulwich gallery, in the midst of a garden, set in

---

[1] Cecilia Novello, a well-known concert singer; married to
Thomas James Serle, the dramatic author.

[2] The Gonsalvi is in Windsor Castle, and is by Lawrence, not
Vandyke.

the midst of a lovely English village! Many a charming dreamy day have Charles and I spent there together. Once I spent a day there with beloved and honoured Charles and Mary Lamb. I shall delight in seeing your Mary's "Comic Mask;" and how very very kind of you to be making that "batch of plaster casts" for us. How we shall dote on them! Charles tried his best to take the impression you desired of the little seal-ring, but though he made several trials, none succeeded. He has therefore forwarded you the ring itself by Mr. Putnam, that you may try if you can succeed better. There are also one or two impressions of other of our seals in the box, that you may see how we have tried and failed. Sulphur did better than plaster, but not perfectly, — our want of skill, I fear. The Trihominate desire kindest remembrances to Mrs. B. and yourself. And I beg you to think of me always as   Your affectionate

M. C. C.

JULY 24, 1851,
CRAVEN HILL COTTAGE, BAYSWATER.

DEAR ENTHUSIAST:

I HAD the pleasure of receiving your kind letter of the 8th last Monday. How truly, in your delighted reminiscence of those visits to the R. A. private views, do you confirm John

Keats's words, "A thing of beauty is a joy forever"! Assuredly the enjoyments of art are
lasting. The sight of a picture, a group of
sculpture, not only brightens that hour in which
we enjoy it, but casts a reflected light through
a long vista of years to come. It abides with you,
a treasured possession of which nothing can
deprive you. I am afraid some of what you say
about the Greek Slave's proportion must be
conceded as true. Charles owns it, so do I, on
reflection. But can it be true that the sculptor
of that figure had the bad taste (to say no worse
of it) to disparage the "statue that enchants the
world"? I will own to you that there are points
about that statue that do not altogether please
me — I hold very much with Leigh Hunt's remarks about it, in his late-published autobiography; but still, there is so much of loveliness
in it, that it seems unworthy, especially in one
who is himself a sculptor of a feminine form, to
pick out its faults. Yes, I have seen Flaxman's
beautiful outlines; they are very fine. But do
you know, Charles and I cannot agree with
you and your Mary in allowing him to be the
Shakespeare of art. With all Flaxman's majesty, he is cold, and where will you find one
line in the "Poet of Poets" that is not instinct
with lifelike warmth?

I thank you for the promised maps of your haunts; they will be delightful to me. Also for the Tassean gems. What a pleasure will they be in themselves, and in the circumstance of their owing their existence in their present form to a pair of loving hands that undertook so long a task from pure enthusiasm and kindly feeling! The shade-stands will be doted on for the same reason; though it was a piece of impudence of which only a modest woman would have been capable to downright ask you to make them for me.

Your account of your Angelo and his mundane loves was very amusing. But the circumstance of his mentioning those " nymphs " to his mother delighted me. The boy who makes a confidante of his mother is secured from getting into mischief. Wise and happy the mother who encourages such confidence from her son. In speaking of the several individual traits perceptible in your two boys, you may well exclaim, " What does it all augur ? " The distinct differences to be traced in members of the same family, with the future fates indicated vaguely thereby, are some of the most curious and interesting speculations possible to a parent.

I am sorry to find that this new proposed dress for women meets with your and Mrs. Balmanno's disapprobation. From what little I have heard of it, it seemed to me to promise well for convenience and comfort, especially in travelling or exploring. When we were at Nice, scrambling about the lovely campagnas and mountain paths in the neighbourhood, I confess I have often uttered an internal anathema against the abominable inconvenience of petticoats, and have actually planned a blouse and trousers for my own wear, should I ever again go on an expedition with my dear menfolk. If you had ever known the irritation of spirit and obstruction of limb consequent upon making your way *petticoated* through aloe hedges and up steep rocky ascents, you would not wonder that a poor unhappy mortal woman should aspire to free herself from those female trammels. Besides, one need n't be one whit the less feminine for donning trousers and abjuring skirts. Charles has often proved that he has not the least fear of my " wearing the —— " either actually or metaphorically! Your mention of the katydid singing in your Ailantus tree thus is charming; it brings so presently to my imagination your actual whereabouts.

And so Jenny Lind is living near to you. Is there not an exquisite charm about her singing ? That divine voice and delightful school! I heard her in two of her characters, and was particularly struck with her delicacy and taste in execution, as well as the purity and sweetness of her tone. Her cadences are perfectly musician-like, so admirably in keeping with the style of the song. We have with us at this moment one of the four most divine voices I ever heard — to wit, Malibran, Miss Stevens, Jenny Lind, and Clara Gigliucci. Though she is my sister, I venture to own to you that hers is the transcendent one of the four, supremely beautiful as the other three are — or were. Malibran's fire, Miss Stevens's rich weighty fulness of tone, Jenny Lind's charm of delicacy, are all present to my recollection; but there is a certain quality in Clara's voice that goes direct to the heart, and while it combines the characteristics of the others, has yet a surpassing beauty of its own, which, in my opinion, renders it the voice of voices. To you, who have not heard her, this must at present seem the partiality of a sister; should you ever hear her, I know that you will admit it to be mere truth.

We are very happy, as you may suppose, just now, in this addition to our family party. The Count and she arrived from Lisbon a week ago, in excellent health and spirits, notwithstanding the odious sea voyage. My youngest sister

Sabilla, also, is paying a visit to England just now. She arrived from Nice about ten days before the Gigliuccis came from Lisbon. The only drawback to our pleasure is that we must part again so soon; for our Trihominate trip to Nice is fixed to take place in a short time, so that we shall have Clara and her husband here during our absence. But thus it is, pleasures are apt to come in heaps when they do come, so that we have to choose between them instead of being able to enjoy them successively. To tell you the truth respecting what you say of Charles's " sweet disposition " in allowing my Enthusiast to write to his daughter-in-love as he does, I rather think Charles takes nearly as much pride and delight in the affectionate tone of those letters as I do. Mind I say nearly, not quite! But the fact is, if there is one thing more than another which peculiarly appeals to his gratification, it is commendation and liking of his little wife. You truly call his a sweet disposition; it is unselfishly, generously happy in the approval of his other self, and it has its only proper reward, — her entire and devoted gratitude.

What kind of weather have you just now? Here it is abominable. How the foreigners must laugh at us poor English people and our climate! Yesterday pouring, to-day pouring. Yesterday all the London world was invited to meet the "distinguished foreigners now visiting us," in the Botanical Gardens. But ye gods, what a day for an *al fresco* fête! It was impossible to hope to go! And as for the Exhibition, with the indomitable spirit of Britons, tribes of country cousins may be seen trudging daily across Hyde Park, with tucked-up or draggle-tailed skirts — oh, those petticoats! — ankle-deep in mud, resolved not to be vanquished by weather. It is terrible! This changeable climate is the only drawback to dear old England, but I own it is a serious one.

With all our united regards for the dear Enthusiast and his dear ones, believe me to be

Your grateful
MARY COWDEN CLARKE.

AUG. 14, 1851,
CRAVEN HILL COTTAGE, BAYSWATER.
MY DEAR ENTHUSIAST:

OUR visit this year to my dear mother and father has been fixed to take place earlier than usual, so early as next Thursday morning at half past two — Wednesday night, rather; you may therefore imagine we are rather in a bustle. Notwithstanding, I cannot leave England without saying a word of good-bye to my kind father-in-love, lest he should write to me during my

absence, and be uneasy at the delay which would
occur in my reply. I thank you very much for
sending me those two highly interesting letters
of Mr. Putnam's. The second arrived by the
morning's post; Alf was so amused with it, that
he had some thoughts of sending the paper to
Mr. Ernest Jones. . . .

Your account of your steamer trip across the
bay, of the glorious beach, the sand smooth and
firm as a floor, with the blue Atlantic rolling in,
and of your feast of raspberries, was perfectly
delicious. It is a curious coincidence that just
as your mention of your enjoyment of raspberries reached me, my sister Clara — when we
dined with her the other day — had some raspberries and cream expressly for me, having remembered it was a favourite dainty of mine years
ago. I wish you could have heard her, last
night; she made this bit of a cottage ring with
her enchanting tones, so full, so loud, and withal
so exquisitely sweet; she sang us some of our
old choicest favourites. We had quite a musical
treat; and so long we hermit Trihominate have
famished in this respect that it was doubly and
trebly dear to us.

We were extremely interested with your mention of Daniel Webster; and that little touch of
yours afterwards.

WEDNESDAY, AUG. 16, 10 A.M. I have just heard the guns of the "Asia" go off,—charmed me.

WEDNESDAY, AUG. 16, 1851. I kept my letter unclosed until to-day, lest a letter might arrive from you that I might acknowledge, but now close in all the hurry of packing. God bless you.

MARY COWDEN CLARKE.

OCT. 9, 1851,
CRAVEN HILL COTTAGE, BAYSWATER.

DEAR ENTHUSIAST:

ON our return home from our delightful two months' Italian holiday, the first thing that struck my eyes on entering our own little snuggery (it was late at night when we arrived from Folkestone) was one of my kind father-in-love's gifts, the cedar tub that stands beneath my cabinet and holds my papers. Then I saw a piled-up heap of letters that had accumulated during our absence and awaited us with greetings from friends, lecture business, etc. Among the pleasant handwritings was yours, my dear sir. Then a little note from Clara, who had just left town for her Manchester engagement, told me where I should find the case from America, the key, etc. Then next morning

[103]

came the delight of opening the case and beholding the glories enshrined within. How am I to
thank you sufficiently, dear father-in-love, for so
handsome, so charming a present? It almost
confuses me as much by its munificence as it enchants me by its kindness and its treasures of art
entertainment. What feasts during the coming
winter evenings you have prepared for your grateful daughter-in-love and her two men-folk! We
shall saturate our eyes with graceful forms and
intellectual associations, and so go to bed in the
finest possible frame for enjoying pleasant dreams.
Thank you a thousand times for so beautiful,
so gracious a thought, as this exquisite little
casket and its contents. At present I am so
overwhelmed with work that I dare not allow
myself more than a peep into each drawer of an
evening, when I feel I have earned a right to an
hour's relaxation; but I am like a heroine of some
fairy story, who hugs herself in the knowledge that
she is possessed of the key of some storehouse of
infinite delights; and this is a delight in itself
during the daytime. The opening of the box
and the coming to each beautifully packed article
was as bewitching as some of those visionary
godfather gift-boxes of childhood. I used to
dream of them in my young castle-in-the-air-
building days; and now in my grown-up days I

am having these dreams realized. A rare happiness to have, in maturity, the actual of one childish ideal! . . .

What a pleasant anecdote that is about your directorship of the dancing academy. I doted on dancing as a girl. I am old enough now, alas, to be able to tell you that I was made very proud once by a compliment from Leigh Hunt on my dancing. A poet's flattery is one of the few kinds of flattery that are not only to be endured, but to be welcomed. We forgive the hyperbole for the sake of the honour and glory.

I do not wonder at Mr. Putnam's papers on the Exhibition being "copied and lauded." They were admirable; the Trihominate were delighted with them, and we thank you very heartily for sending us copies, and enabling us to enjoy them.

You interest me highly with your account of the original unpublished letter of Burns on the subject of women. There was a glow, a fervour of feeling in him respecting them, that all but extenuates some of his errors toward them, and that makes all he says in their honour of the warmest interest to one of their own sex. Is this letter likely to be given to the world in print? If so, I shall beseech a copy of my father-in-love's kindness.

Why, my dear sir, will you apologize for

"perpetually flying off in such incoherent transitions," as you call it, in your letters? It is their very freedom and playful ease that make them so peculiarly pleasant. You and I *gossip* to each other — not *write*. A staid, formal letter is a troublesome affair indeed, both to write and to read. "Thou and I are too wise to write coherently."

What lovely gems are those two copies of exquisite, charming, amiable Correggio you have sent me! I have put one in my miniature Shakespeare (opposite the passage — "Who can sever love from charity?" Pickering's edition) and the other I shall keep for my mother's. I am to make her an illustrated edition of my own, crammed full of pictures, like a child's book. It was a long promise, and was to have been done on my concluding the Concordance; but time — time — time — when shall I find enough for all I have to do? No wonder your C. H. friend tried to hoax you with a spurious portrait of your "darling," since you played off so successful a "bam" upon him! How can you expect to escape, you who are so wicked in the same kind yourself? Do you know, I am charmed with your dog's name. It is truly poetical. Whose thought was it? Yours or your Mary's, of course.

Your going to awaken poor Kelpie[1] when he moans in his sleep is just what I fancy of you; and the account of your writing at night, and breathing the open air, and revelling in the moonlight at intervals, enchants me. This is the sort of feelings and pursuits you cultivate so wisely, and which will do more than anything to keep you going and abate the regrets that *will* occasionally beset us for the youth that cannot return. Give my love to Mrs. Balmanno, and tell her I thank her cordially for what you tell me of her sympathy and comprehension respecting the writing of those tales. You say, " If you rise so early, when do you retire? " You will laugh when I tell you that, though a Londoner, I like to " lie down with the lamb." What will you say to the Trihominate when I tell you that they generally go to bed at ten? We work so hard all day, and begin so early, that we are glad of early hours at night. This makes us dread parties, and accept of as few invitations as possible. We are terrible hermits.

I remember the Gonsalvi you speak of. It is Lawrence's portrait of Cardinal Gonsalvi, — a wonderful face of keen and astute intelligence, — in the St. George's Hall, or the anteroom, at

---

[1] Mr. Balmanno's dog.

Windsor Castle. Charles says he thought Bentivoglio[1] was Titian's. I'll tell you a portrait that is a great love of mine; it is in Hampton Court: Alessandro de' Medici, by Titian. It is quite an Italian head — regular features, beautiful dark olive complexion, a countenance full of thought and intellectual refinement. The hand holds a book, with the forefinger pressed within the leaves, as if to keep a passage open ready for referring to again when it has been thoroughly considered; it evidently occupies him now. Some of these portraits of the old Italian masters are more suggestive, more comprehensive, than many a historical picture full of figures, and I would infinitely rather have them for companions. At the same time there are some which, for their very force, I would not have constantly near me for any consideration. For instance, the portrait of Ignatius Loyola, the founder of the Jesuits, by Titian, would give me a nervous fever to have by me night and day, I verily believe. It would be like being haunted by an evil spirit as bad as poor Gretchen in the church, during the " Dies Irae ; " it would prompt all sorts of dark and evil imaginings, fruitless remorse, vain regrets.

---

[1] The Bentivoglio is by Vandyke, and is in the Pitti Palace.

Your second letter is dated Aug. 10th. It was the very day we arrived in Nice, finding my dear mother well, thank God, though she had been poorly a day or two before. We spent a charming holiday with her and my dear father. Do you know, you were exquisitely associated and present with us, each time my dear mother and I drove out together, which we frequently did. She is not a very stout walker now, and as air and exercise are essential, Alfred makes it his privilege to provide her with a little carriage in which she can be driven out along the shores of the Mediterranean. Well, as she and I used to sit side by side, talking over all our thousand and one subjects of chat, and inhaling the soft southern air that comes wafted across the waters, warmed by an Italian sun, yet tempered by the sea and mountain breeze, together with this "spiced air," I used to find mingled with it the delicious cedar scent that is now so intimately connected in my mind with you and your kind gifts. The fact is, my dear mother's shawl lies in the cedar case, and is exquisitely scented in consequence. I sent her over the cedar case, knowing how fond she is of this scent, —indeed, like most persons of delicate organization, she is keenly alive to the pleasures of sweet odours, — and it stands in her dressing-room and holds her furs, shawls, etc. So you see you often accompanied us in our drives. . . . Sometimes we used to have a laugh, when my raptures at finding myself with her again made me forget that we were still in the Nice streets, and I'd cuddle her arm or fondle her hand. She said they would see how her English children ill used her.

You grieve me to find you have actually ordered a copy to be made for me of your lovely ivory gem. My dear sir, you are too generous; you will make me chary of expressing my interest and admiration in any of your art possessions which you describe to me. I should have been more than contented had you indulged me with a sight of it, as you have promised; but to have a duplicate made of it is carrying your indulgence to your daughter-in-love too far; you will spoil her. You are too kind, too lavish in your gifts; I feel really ashamed to accept it.

Your account of the artist and his conjugal vexations was very amusingly told. How good of you to console him! Very many thanks to you for your minute description of the plaster-cast process. I shall not fail to impart it to my sister Emma, and to give her your kind presents on her return to town. She is at present on a visit to an aunt in Devonshire.

I can precisely understand what you say about your preferring simple songs to Italian music; it is a frequent taste with those who are no musicians, but have a soul for music. How you would dote upon hearing Clara sing a Scotch song, without accompaniment, which she learned in Scotland. I think the words begin " O that my love were yon red rose!" It goes direct to the heart, so simple in itself, so exquisite in her full, rich, cordial voice. And you should hear her sing that Jacobite song, "Bonnie Prince Charlie." It's enough to tear your soul out of your body, and make you snatch up a sword and go out and fight, for pure loyalty and devotion. Once at Berlin, when Lord William Russell, brother to our prime minister, Lord John, was ambassador there, she was at a party at his house, and on his asking her for an encore to a Scotch song, she saucily substituted " Awa, *whigs*, awa!" which of course enchanted him with the pleasant impudence of the jest. So you see she does sing Scottish ballads; although I dare say she would be much obliged to you for your promised additional hints in the true pronunciation. I don't wonder at your calling her by her Christian name, everybody does. We don't say Mr. Shakespeare — darling Willie, dear William, beloved Will.

I should certainly have followed your suggestion in taking some of the duplicates of the gems
to my dear mother, had they arrived before we
left England; but as it is I shall hope to have
the pleasure next year, if I go. How beautifully
they were packed! How kind of you, dear father-
in-love! What dainty cotton that is which you
put with them. It is so white, so delicate, that
I think of making myself a quilted white satin
bonnet with some of it. Ask Mrs. B. if she does
not agree with me that a quilted white satin bonnet trimmed with swansdown is very pretty winter
wear. If she says yes, I shall wish I were near
neighbour enough of hers to quilt her one myself.
God bless you, dear sir. May He send you many
years of health, happiness, and prosperity, prays,
in all sincerity, your affectionate daughter-in-
love

M. C. C.

Charles has just told me that he has seen in a
shop window an admirable portrait of your friend
Mr. Burton, in the character of Captain Cuttle.
He says it is very spirited and clever. I forgot
to ask you whether the box of Italian fruits,
which my mother tells me she had shipped from
Nice for New York, at the beginning of the summer, has reached you yet.

JANUARY 1ST, 1852.

" The very firstlings of my heart shall be
The firstlings of my hand."

CRAVEN HILL COTTAGE, BAYSWATER.

GIVE me joy, my dear sir : I yesterday wrote
the last line of the fifteen stories; and now
I will confess to you that I had my fears, if I took
my Nice holiday last autumn, I might have found
it impossible to complete my task in time. But
it is accomplished, *Deo gratias!*

The year concluded in a most wondrous
way; it was a year of marvels, you know; the
Exhibition to wit! I received a note by the
early post from a gentleman in America, a
most dear and enthusiastic friend of mine, containing the most mysterious hints of a surpassing
glory and triumph, "an honour that I dreamed
not of," an honour that it would have been wild
to have dreamed of, an honouring compliment
from America to England — from American
gentlemen to an English woman — a national
compliment, no less than an individual one. . . .
The note seemed to imply that she ought already
to be in possession of this same tribute; however, the delight was none the less for the spice
of mystery that was thus thrown around the
matter, for in all probability the chair alluded to
in the note would soon arrive. Well, in the

8 [113]

course of the morning a gentleman left a card. This proved to be Mr. G. Landell, who subsequently — that very afternoon — wrote to say that he had received a communication from Mr. Balmanno of New York, respecting the gratifying testimonial from citizens of the United States, and would feel greatly obliged if Mrs. C. C. would permit him to make a drawing of the chair and desk for illustration in the " Ladies' Journal and Pictorial Times." More confirmation of this miraculous "glory and triumph." I of course wrote to say I should be charmed to accord the permission for the drawing when the "sitter" arrived. . . .

Your usual modesty and kind generosity desires that I will not express my acknowledgments to you for the share you have had in bringing about this most proud event.[1] . . . Only Shakespeare's own words could be strong enough; let me borrow them on this occasion: " Time as long again would be filled up, my brother, with our thanks; and yet we should, for perpetuity, go hence in debt." [2]

And now let me endeavour to acknowledge with some order your several kind communications since my return from Nice. One, dated

---

[1] The presentation of the testimonial chair.
[2] " The Winter's Tale," Act I, Scene II.

the 26th of Oct., reached me on Lord Mayor's day. It afforded a rather curious confirmation of what I have told you of the beautiful regularity of your handwriting. I had given my damsels — they are from the country and therefore peculiarly interested with such a London sight — leave to go and see the civic show. Accordingly, I was playing Betty for the nonce, and hearing the postman's ring at the garden gate bell, I ran down. In the postbox, through its glass side, I discerned a letter lying, and seeing what I thought straight printed lines through the envelope, ejaculated, "Pshaw, a stupid circular, I suppose!" when on turning to the address I recognized my dear Enthusiast's hand. . . .

You enquire whether Charles reads my letters to you, as he would then have a higher opinion, etc. The fact is, Charles has had an infinity of my letters, such as they are. We are never absent from each other, but we write to one another every day, minutely; and even when we have anything particularly hateful to communicate, we set it down in shorthand. However, to reply directly to your question, I do read him some of my letters to you, when I think there is any gossip in which he will feel interested, and he enjoys all your very kind and pleasant letters to me.

Your next received is dated Nov. 18, and contains the distressing intelligence of your having been ill of a fever. But your subsequent letter making no allusion to indisposition, I have hoped that you are quite recovered. I have not seen the volume you mention of the "Sentiments and Similes," only noticed such a book has been advertised as a Christmas gift book. The illustrator is Mr. Humphreys, whom I met at Mrs. Loudon's, and whose name is down for Sir Lucius O'Trigger in the bill of "The Rivals" that I sent you, performed at her house. I remember he was a very gentlemanly man, and played the character extremely well. I thank you for what you tell me of the volumes of "Girlhood" having been printed on larger paper, etc. It is pleasant to be in such liberal hands as Mr. Putnam's.

No, my dear sir, I did not happen to see or hear of the book-tray at the Exhibition, which you mention; but there were hosts of beautiful things there that I missed, as I suppose many others did. It was a glorious event. I suppose you heard of the banner with those lines from our Idol, "Our revels now are ended," etc., having been hung from one of the galleries on the closing day. Charles and I were present; you may be sure our eyes were moistened at the

sight. And the effect of the multitudinous voice
in "God save the Queen," that was sung on that
occasion, was impressive, even though the size of
the building rendered it impossible that it should
be harmoniously executed. Some sang in one
key, some in another; yet somehow the effect of
the whole was just that beauty of unison in feeling which is so fine and impressive. Have you
found the "begun letter" you mention? Pray
finish and send it. It will be interesting, from
its having been commenced before you took the
fever.

Alfred duly received a copy of the newspaper
containing an account of the St. Andrew's festival, and a transcript of those two fine songs of
Mrs. Balmanno's. We were perfectly charmed
with them; so free, so animated, so full of spirit
and feeling; they are beautiful. You must be
very proud of so true a poetess, in so sweet and
gentle and womanly a wife as your little treasure
of a Mary must be. Like a true genius, she
seems to be as modest as she is gifted. You say,
at the conclusion of this note of Nov. 18th, " Of
course you are acquainted with ' Tam O'Shan-
ter.'" Of course! I wish you could hear my
Charles read it! Although you are a Scotchman born, yet I dare to wish you could hear him
read that great comic poem to a sympathizing

audience. It is really admirable, because he himself admires and enjoys it so thoroughly.

And now I come to your yesterday's letter. But I despair of doing justice to the feelings with which I read the hint of what honour has been paid your daughter-in-love; therefore I refrain, and content myself with thanking you heartily for your great kindness in sending me that copy of dear Burns's letter. Be assured, I shall take the utmost care that it shall not be re-transcribed.

You make Charles and me on tiptoe of expectation with respect to the Shakespeare papers you mention, and of which you have so very kindly and thoughtfully sent us a copy in the magazines, through Mr. Chapman. This very day I received a letter in which there was this delightfully cordial passage about our Idol: " He fills a place between men and angels, but I doubt if an angel could have written as well on matters that relate to mere humanity. I hope that you will not think I mean in this remark to speak at all profanely. It is not that I think less of angels but more of Shakespeare." Is not this sterling? Your daughter-in-love wrote back word: " Be assured, nothing that could be said of Shakespeare's divinity would appear profanity to yours faithfully and obliged, M. C. C."

The man who wrote thus was J. Payne Collier. His behaviour to me many years ago — *vide* preface to Concordance, you know — was worthy a genuine Shakespeare-lover, as he is. And on the only one occasion that I saw him (it was in the green room of the Haymarket Theatre when I was dressed for the part of Mistress Quickly) he said in a way worthy of a knight of old, or of my Enthusiast himself, "Let me kiss the hand that wrote the Concordance." I make no apology for repeating this to my father-in-love, for his own enthusiasm sanctions it; and besides, it reflects honour on Mr. Collier himself.

While I have been writing, a friend of ours has been here. Charles has a troublesome attack of rheumatism, which confines him to his room just now, and Dr. Storrar kindly attends him, — Dr. Storrar of Helena, you know, — and being a Scotch gentleman, I knew he would appreciate Mrs. Balmanno's songs. He read them aloud, and, with his wife, was charmed with them. He particularly praised their vigour and spirit, which chiefly struck myself, in *him*. It is one of the glorious privileges of art that it can thus communicate the strongest of sympathetic pleasures between people hundreds of miles apart. Here were we enjoying Mrs. Balmanno's ideas as forcibly and as keenly, with the wide Atlantic rolling between her and us, as though we saw her face and heard her speak the words. The Storrars are very kind and intimate friends of ours. Mrs. Storrar owns herself an adorer of "Clarkey." So she and her good husband came up into our room and chatted with us about all sorts of pleasant things, that made us almost forget that "Clarkey," as she calls him, is an invalid. And from Mrs. Balmanno's songs we went on to "A man's a man for a' that," and we had out some of Robert Burns's delicious songs, until we had eyes and hearts full. You will probably have seen the new edition of Shakespeare called "The Lansdowne Shakespeare." It is a very handsome volume, is it not? And the red printing for the names and stage directions looks very elegant, as well as distinct. . . .

JAN. 2. Yesterday afternoon I received your packet sent through His Excellency, Abbott Lawrence. If I found it difficult to express my feelings before, what must be my speechless condition now, since I have read all those overwhelming testimonials of the active kindness and affectionate interest of my dear father-in-love! Well may he have given himself that title. . . . But let me tell you how it all happened; as Charlotte Grandison says, "I love to write to the moment."

While I was finishing the above scribble to you,

a card was brought up to me from a gentleman who was waiting to see me, — Mr. Charles F. Dennet, — and with the card was your packet and your letters, the handwriting of which I of course instantly recognized. I went to Mr. Dennet, and found a most gentlemanly, handsome young man, who very courteously informed me that the testimonial chair had arrived at Mr. Lawrence's, and that my further wishes upon the disposition of the gift from America were to be consulted. I assure you, my dear father-in-love, I felt perfectly overwhelmed; the honour was so distinguished, so unprecedented, I scarcely knew what to say or to propose. Finally, Mr. Dennet most kindly and considerately agreed to call here this morning and see my brother Alfred. This morning he has done so, and they are just gone together to Piccadilly, that my brother may be presented to Mr. Lawrence and learn his wishes on the subject, as they will of course guide mine, as to the mode in which I shall receive the honoured gift from America. How shall I thank you, my kind father-in-love, for all the loving pains you have taken to make this presentation a source of multiplied pleasure to me, — the autograph letters containing such valued tributes of kind sympathy and encouragement from several of America's most revered names; that most noble letter of Mr. Webster's; the proof impressions, the lists of names and states, all so affectionately arranged and packed as to contribute more to my delight! Dear sir, and do you know, what touched me to the heart was the *sentiment* of your sending that identical little gold coin that had passed through the hands of that noble great man. It seemed hardly a piece of money, but rather some valued medal and token of national and individual kindness and esteem. I feel inclined to have it hung as an ornament to a bracelet or some such article of wear, that I may keep it about me ; only that I should not like to have it drilled or injured. It was a most sweet thought, your preserving that actual coin, as a type of all the other donations and a relic of the high-minded man himself.

As to your own letter (this is doubtless the one begun before your fever) of explanation and minute information, conveying so heartfelt an evidence of the kind interest you take in your grateful daughter-in-love, I could not read it through without weeping tears of mingled gratification and tenderness. I was obliged to pause several times, to regain my voice, as I read it to Charles. In the evening, I had a repetition of the pleasure of looking through the proud contents of the packet, and rereading your letter, when Alfred returned home. I walked to meet him before dinner, according to my daily practice for health's sake; and as I passed through the open air, with nothing but the cope of heaven above between America and my thoughts, you may believe how fervently they breathed gratitude and blessings toward her and the warm generous hearts that had sent so glorious a token of sympathy and commendation toward the humble little Englishwoman who had worked in the cause in common with herself. This gracious commencement of my New Year I owe to my venerated father-in-love; God bless him for the beautiful idea in the first instance, and for having carried it through so perseveringly, energetically, and effectively.

My poor Charles, in his painful attack of rheumatism, has found a most agreeable solace from this surpassing honour to his little woman. Between the paroxysms he revels in the kind expressions, and amongst his groans has smiles and enjoyment for the pleasant testimonies. I have just made him laugh, by reading him the above. He dictates all kinds of cordial things on his behalf to his *father-in-love-in-law!*

I shall not detain this letter, as this is American post day; but I mean to write my acknowledgments to each of these subscribers to the testi-

monial, and shall send you the heap of letters
with their envelopes, and thus tax still farther
your trouble in this matter to forward them to
their respective destinations. So you see, your
occupation is far from being gone! I think of
writing a general letter of thanks to them all
collectively, of which copies can be sent to each;
and besides, a letter of personal acknowledgment,
from myself to every one, since I fortunately am
acquainted (thanks to your kind and thoughtful
provision) with their respective names. How
particularly considerate and good of you it was
to append those little annotations and the several autograph letters you so generously sent!
They enabled me so delightfully to individualize
the different writers. Let me know, my dear
sir, whether you think the above-mentioned proposed letters will answer the purpose you desire
for Mr. —— and Mr. Tefft and Miss Quincy;
if not, I shall have great pleasure in writing them
an especial little supplementary note each. Pray,
if at any time you should again wish for such
a thing, ask without hesitation. . . . Meantime,
with affectionate remembrances to Mrs. Balmanno, and kindly greetings to Mr. Angelo,
believe me to be

Your grateful

MARY COWDEN CLARKE.

I have forgotten to mention that my brother Alfred would feel particularly obliged to you if you could obtain him any information — printed particulars or others — respecting postal communication with America; especially how, in the general opinion, the new American Postal Act has succeeded in its working. He wants it for the new campaign against the "taxes on knowledge," which it is hoped will be final.

JAN. 15, 1852,
CRAVEN HILL COTTAGE.

MY DEAR FATHER-IN-LOVE:

I WILL not delay another post, although I am unable yet to tell you I have seen the chair. On Monday last, the son of His Excellency, Abbott Lawrence — Colonel Lawrence — called here with a very handsome letter of official presentation, and very kindly and considerately told me that the chair should have come that same day, but the weather being so very inclement, Mr. Lawrence had thought it best to send it next day. Ever since then we have had the same miserable weather, incessant rain, which I suppose is the reason why the packing-case has not arrived. But I thought, as to-morrow will be American post day, I would send my letter of acknowledgment without delay, that Mr. Lawrence might forward it, if he thought proper, at once. Alf is now gone off in a cab to Piccadilly, with the letter to His Excellency, and the packet containing the several letters to the subscribers enclosed to you, as Alf will ask the favour that it may go through the ambassador's bag. Yesterday I wrote my heap of letters, never stirring till I had finished them every one; and — as a proof to you how kind my men-folk are to your "darling" — when Alf and Charles came home, the one from a public meeting and the other from lecturing at the City of London Institution, they both set to and helped me, — they folding and I directing, until the whole were finished. It was past twelve ere we had concluded. Think of that rakishness, for the hermit Trihominate!

I write upon a sheet of the paper containing the printed copy of my letter of thanks, that you may see it at once in case the packet containing the rest should be delayed. But I have left them all open, so that you may see what I have said to each, if the father-in-love's partiality prompts him to take sufficient interest in them. . . . There is one big thing I must ask you to do, and that is to let me know the amount of those certain disbursements of postage, etc., which this task will entail. I will be beholden to you for the trouble, but ought not to allow you to defray the filthy lucre. After all, you will most probably laugh at me for my being scrupulous about such a trifle, when I have received such unpayable things at your hands. But fathers are content to let their spoiled daughters encroach, and be ever the obliged party. I sometimes tell my own father and mother, " I have owed you first the inestimable boon of existence, then the benefits and delights of a liberal education, and I am constantly incurring fresh debts of love and kindness ; so I must e'en rest satisfied to be the eternally obliged and eternally grateful." And so to you, dear father-in-love, I can only say, " I thankfully rest your debtor." . . . Oh! The Trihominate of course drank your health in bumpers the very first time Charles was well enough to come downstairs to dinner. He is getting better slowly, but I trust surely. We were all three particularly struck with the admirable manner in which you drew up the account of the testimonial — for doubtless it was your kind doing ? — which appeared in the " Lady's Newspaper." It has been copied since in the " Manchester Exchange " and " Times " at full length. I was particularly touched with the extreme delicacy and tact with which my dear kind father-in-love kept his own large share of the transaction, and even his own

name, completely out of sight. It was doubly
and trebly generous. . . .

My brain and hands have been so full with
work and happiness and honour that I have had
no leisure yet to look into the papers, though I
have received the magazines containing them
quite safely. I deeply grieve at the derogation
of Charles Halpin. And to think what his poor
father would have felt on all accounts, could he
have foreseen it!

One of the pleasant letters I have had touching this distinguished gift from America came
from France. Here is one sentence which I
know will please my Enthusiast: " Ma voix est
bien faible, mais elle compte sur les cordes qui,
dans une organization comme la sienne, ne per-
dront jamais leur sonorité. Mon Dieu! Comme
ta bonne mère doit pleurer de joie." He claims
brotherhood with me, we having known each
other from childhood. Hence the familiarity of
" thee and thou " between us.

M. C. C.

January 30th, 1852,
Craven Hill Cottage, Bayswater.

My dear Father-in-love:

THIS week has been rich in letters to me
from you. First, I received by post yours
of January 10; second, the note of January 7,

enclosed in parcel of magazines; and third, your hurried few lines dated January 17th, written just in time to save the English mail, and enclosing the letter to Mrs. Sinclair. Just like your kind heart to write that warm assurance to the anxious mother. Thank God, the right of the injured innocence you have with so manly an earnestness espoused is in a fair way to triumph, as it should. I trust your next accounts will bring word that legally, as well as virtually, she is cleared, and that she is safely released from bondage with so base a ruffian. Curiously enough, the very day before your letter arrived, in looking over some papers, I came upon a scrap cut from a paper at the time — I think the "Examiner" — and on the back of the extract which I cut out happens to be part of a critique of this very man's acting. As I think it will make you smile, — it did us, for I read it aloud to my men-folk, — I transcribe it here:

"Our old friend Mr. Forrest afforded great amusement to the public by his performance of Macbeth on Friday week, at the Princess's. Indeed, our best comic actors do not often excite so great a quantity of mirth. The change from an inaudible murmur to a thunder of sound was enormous; but the grand feature was the combat, in which he stood scraping his sword against that of Macduff. We were at a loss to know what this gesture meant, till an enlightened critic in the gallery shouted out, 'That's right! Sharpen it!'"

It is too late, my dear father-in-love, for me to obey your injunction respecting the letters of acknowledgment. You will doubtless have received them ere this through the ambassador's bag, and I hope when you have seen them you will approve. Well, and now that I have actually beheld the chair I feel more than ever at a loss to express my admiration and delight. Its beauty even surpasses what I had imagined it would be, although your graphic description of it led me to form very superb notions. It is exquisite in all respects, such artistic taste in the design of the carving and ornaments especially. As for the satin brocade, it is at once so rich and so delicate, that I hardly like — I who seldom wear anything but black — to sit down upon it. It seems too fairly gorgeous for every-day use. At present it remains in the centre of our little parlour, like a throne, for the admiration of all our friends who come and look at it. Alf talks of flying off with it for a time, to his house of business in the City, where it may be exhibited for the more extensive beholding of his numerous connection, who take an interest in the family and their honours. He has already, like a kind

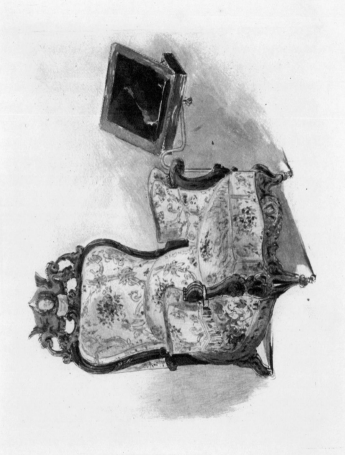

brother as he is, sent off to France nearly two hundred copies of the "Lady's Newspaper" containing the first account, and as many of the numbers containing the picture of the testimonial chair. Of course, Mr. Landell has sent you copies?

Thank you very much for your kind present of the American edition of my "Blue-coat Girls." And will you do me the favour to convey my best acknowledgments to Mr. Putnam, who kindly sent me two more copies lately. It is delightful to see my large family of daughters — more than fifteen, for some of them are twins — so gracefully dressed and handsomely provided for in their Transatlantic costume.

You will smile — and yet no, you have a corner in your heart that will bid you understand and sympathize with my feelings — when I tell you that one of the things that peculiarly charmed me on unpacking the precious gift was to find that holland cover put with it. This little circumstance showed such kindly thought, so considerate an intention, that it touched me especially. . . .

Charles has read aloud to me the first Halpin paper. It does indeed establish gloriously the fact of our Idol's supremacy in learning, as in all else. But his works themselves bear intrinsic

testimony to the truth. So far, I am not excited
to such enthusiastic rejoicing by the papers,
because ever since I have been able to comprehend Shakespeare's own writings, I have felt
convinced on the point, in my own mind. Still,
it is delightful to have it proclaimed aloud to
the world, who have been too much accustomed
hitherto to acquiesce in the verdict of Jonson's
envious "little Latin and less Greek." Whoever notes some of Shakespeare's words, created
by himself for his own peculiar use, cannot
fail to perceive that he must be a classical
scholar. Have we not "*cadent* tears," "*inten-
ible* sieve," "a *pudency* so rosy," "*crescive* in his
faculty," and scores of others, to prove that he
knew how to anglicize a Latin word when he
wanted an expressive one for his purpose, not
already in his mother tongue? I have often
longed to write a paper on this subject; but, like
other odd scraps of purposes never fulfilled, it
has gone to increase the mosaic pavement of
Pandemonium.

There is a passage in your letter of Dec. 5th,
'51, that I have many times reread with heartfelt joy. This is it:

"I am still hearty and strong as a lion; witness
thereto my two-mile race down Broadway from Niblo's
tavern, at two o'clock in the morning, on Monday

night, after attending the festival of St. Andrew. It was a bitter night, cold as Nova Zembla, but the moon shone bright as day, and I was warm with wine, but sober as St. Andrew."

Glorious! Bravissimo! . . .

M. C. C.

MAR. 25TH, 1852,
27 PORCHESTER TERRACE, BAYSWATER.

MY DEAR FATHER-IN-LOVE:

ARE you not surprised to observe by my new date that we have taken flight from the nest on Craven Hill? But I had long fore-seen that this building mania in our neighbour-hood must perforce sooner or later turn us out from our sunny nook. Fortunately, our flight has been no farther than to a cottage at the end of our garden, abutting on the very premises; still, to me, an old bird, a very nightingale or raven for clinging to one particular spot, the removal has been a serious affair. As beloved Charles Lamb says, "My household goods plant a terribly fixed foot and are not to be rooted up without blood." One of my pleas-antest counterbalances came to me in the midst of my turmoil, in the shape of your most welcome letter dated Feb. 15th and 20th. It chanced to reach me on the very evening on which I slept for the first time in our new domicile; and it came to me like a paternal blessing, to hallow and accompany me into my new abode. Thank you earnestly, dear sir, for it. I like immensely your idea of the banquet to be given to the enthusiastic Mr. Burton (please tell him that I once enjoyed a very happy week at Cambridge, soon after my marriage, with my father and mother and husband; and that when we visited Milton's college, where you say Mr. Burton studied, and were shown the tree said to have been planted by the glorious poet in the college garden, Charles took his hat reverently off as he stood beneath its boughs, much to the amazement of a matter-of-fact fellow who was showing us the lions), and shall hope to hear of all these hilarious proceedings on the occasion of the 23rd April. . . .

I knew you would be amused with that scrap about Forrest, and therefore I sent it to you; but do not "make good use of it by and by," keep it snugly to yourself. He is not worth attacking or annoying; that would be too much like treating him *in his own style*.

Charles is absent from home on a long lecture tour in the North. He has been spending some delightful time in your beautiful Edinburgh, and been most warmly received by its kindly inhabitants. It is a thing to be proud of, being cordially received there; for they rank as fastidious judges. But they not only made a darling of him in the lecture room; they welcomed him into their society, and caused him to meet some of their most distinguished literary people. And all this, you may imagine, not a little rejoiced the heart of his "little woman." It has been even a more delightful visit than his former one there, and that was highly gratifying.

In one of his letters from Edinburgh, replying to one of mine in which I told him of the receipt of your last delightful one just at the period of my entering our new abode, he bids me tell you — but I will quote his own words: " Tell your kind Enthusiast that I have sent no message about this magnificent tribute of honour to the one of this earth that I love beyond myself, and only live for; but my silence is to be attributed to anything but indifference. I wish he could know the amount of my pride at the glory that has streamed upon her across the Atlantic, and the number of times that the whole transaction, with its splendid results, has seethed in my mind. I say it with the most devout truth, that I am three hundred and sixty degrees — the entire circle — more cordially happy at the honour having been paid to her than if three hundred and sixty times its amount in applause and pecuniary value had been paid to myself."

I had a very polite letter from Mr. S. Austin Allibone of Philadelphia, the other day, acknowledging my letter of thanks to him as one of the subscribers to the testimonial chair. Are you personally acquainted with him?

You will be pleased to learn, my dear father-in-love, that your daughter-in-love had a most handsome communication from the Shakespeare Society in acknowledgment of the dedication to them of her story of " Imogen." I cannot refrain from making an extract from the secretary's— Mr. Tomlins's — letter : " A most unanimous sentiment of gratitude and admiration was expressed for the services you have rendered to the lovers of Shakespeare (which is nearly equivalent to saying, that you have rendered to everybody), by the various modes in which you have illustrated his writings, more especially by that truly noble monument, your Concordance of his works. Our worthy Director and Chairman, Mr. J. Payne Collier, declared he considered it more valuable than all the notes of all the commentators." Ah, my dear sir, do not these last words smite you with a little remorse of conscience? You see how he takes public occasion to do honour to your daughter-in-love ; and yet you could go out of your way to give him an unkind dig, at the very time you were kindly doing all you could to glorify her yourself. But I am visited now with a little remorse of conscience myself, for having come to the conclusion of my letter with something akin to a reproach. Let us exchange forgiveness and continue to think of me, as I am in truth,

Your grateful

MARY COWDEN CLARKE.

Love to Mrs. Balmanno.

APRIL 19TH, 1852,

27 PORCHESTER TERRACE, BAYSWATER.

MY DARLING FATHER-IN-LOVE :

ON Saturday Mr. Dennet obligingly brought me your packets through favour of the ambassador's bag. . . . I shall imagine you are "ironing me," as Fielding's Mrs. Slipslop says, if you talk of "generosity" in sending you those trifles I had the pleasure of forwarding. If there is a quality which I recognize in myself with some degree of approval, and conviction that I possess it, perseverance is that quality. I remember that, oddly enough, while I was entering the town of Stratford-upon-Avon when Charles and I visited it in 1846, — he was engaged to lecture

there, and took me with him, a high treat, as you
may suppose, — I was haunted with that line
of Ulysses in " Troilus and Cressida : " " Perseverance, dear my lord, keeps honour bright."[1]
And when I told Charles my fancy, he laughed
and called me a conceited creature; though in
all honesty and sincerity of truth, I was utterly
unconscious of the latent vanity which might
have lurked in the association and prompted the
haunting memory of the words at that particular
juncture. Thanks for your promise of "keeping
quiet a little while longer."

About a week ago I received a remittance on
account, from Mr. Putnam, which I have acknowledged.

And so you are apt to be impatient and irri-
table, are you, you wicked Enthusiast ? So
much so, as to goad your gentle wife, with her
smiling eyes, — I think I see her look, — to call
you M. C. C.'s Testy-Monial ? Fie upon you !
But you say you shall consider it a kindness in
me to lecture you on every and any subject
when I think you deserve it. Pray remember
I am no lecturer, only a lecturer's wife ! You
exclaim, " Jealous ? Lord love you, darling,
was there ever a true, whole-souled lover

---

[1] Act III, Scene III.

that was not?" Now, can you ask that seriously? And yet, I know it is one of the fallacies in principle held by you men as a truth in love-ethics, that jealousy is a proof of love. Monstrous! I could write a volume to bear testimony that it is a proof of *self-love;* and that freedom from jealousy in a pure lover is the surest voucher for the truth and force of his affections. But enough of this, I must not weary you with my whimsical theories. . . .

What you say of the reality of the signature to the Concordance preface tempts me to tell you the history of the said signing, as it may make my father-in-love smile at another instance of his daughter's perseverance. When that first edition had to receive my name, I went down to the printing office early, as I had often done before when I wanted anything particularly stated about proofs, etc. It was a little dingy room, up a flight of stairs in Ivy Lane, Paternoster Row, just beneath the grand shadow of venerable St. Paul's Cathedral. I stuck to my work, the printer's devils supplying me from time to time with armfuls of prefaces in sheets, open at the right spot for affixing my signature. Hour after hour I heard boom forth from glorious old Paul's deep-toned bell, and still, on I worked. Mr. Manning (he was the partner of

Mason at that time) came very courteously, in the course of the morning, to ask me if I would have lunch; but I wanted to complete my task, and declined. Afternoon drew on, the shadows in the dingy little room deepened and deepened, until it became too dark to see to write any longer. I was sitting in the dusk, patiently waiting till the time for lighting the gas should arrive, when I heard a step coming up the stairs: it was Mr. Manning returning from his dinner. It makes me laugh now to recall the tone of amazement in which he exclaimed, when he discerned me, "You here still!" *But I got them all done at that one sitting.*

I am sorry to say I cannot tell you who is the author of that saying, "There is but one step from the sublime to the ridiculous."[1] I see the question is mooted in that copy of the "Literary World," which reached me, addressed in your handwriting. . . .

Many thanks for the papers containing that appeal relative to the Honourable Daniel Webster's election to the Presidency; and for the

---

[1] This saying has been attributed to Fontenelle; to Thomas Paine, who writes in his "Age of Reason," "One step above the sublime makes the ridiculous, and one step above the ridiculous makes the sublime again;" and to Napoleon Buonaparte, who said, "Du sublime au ridicule, il n'y a qu'un pas."

one giving the account of the meeting in honour
of Fenimore Cooper, and Mr. Bryant's admirable discourse upon his writings and genius.
I had the delight of reading it aloud to my
Charles, who, with myself, was charmed with its
manly tone, its fulness of justice to the subject,
and its able achievement altogether.

Since I last wrote to you I have had the pleasure of perusing a volume of Bryant's collected
poems. I was greatly struck with his purity of
taste, his genuine adoration of nature, and his
peculiar revelling in the breezy air. This love
of the open, fresh winds of heaven imparts an
especial vigour and freshness to the style of his
poetry. Above all the pieces in the book, I
most particularly admire and take to my heart of
hearts the one entitled " A Forest Hymn." It
is full of highest and truest religion, a genuine
devotional fervour. The one called " The Evening Wind " is also most delicious in its union of
simplicity with imagination. The image of the
sleeping child with its " moistened curls " is perfect in its truth to nature. It is only your true
poet who will venture on such truth. Shakespeare was not afraid of the " pearly sweat, resem-
bling dew of night," in that exquisite picture of
his Lucrece in her chaste bed.

I received a note — enclosing one from you,

dated Sept. 5th, 1851 — from General Swift, about a week since. His own polite communication was as follows :

"With deep respect for the character and achievements of Mrs. Cowden Clarke, added to admiration, General Swift more than regrets that he is prevented, by unavoidable summons to the country, the honour of calling in person to present the accompanying note from his friend Balmanno. It were superfluous to assure Mrs. Clarke of the high value which all readers of the almost superhuman Bard, in the United States, do entertain for herself individually, and as the best friend of the memory of the 'sweet swan.' Mrs. Clarke must have heard the oft-repeated and grateful thanks from across the sea.

"LONDON, 12TH APRIL, 1852."

.   .   .   .

Your graphic description of your scene with Mrs. Forrest was indeed most entertaining. I think her plan of attack and the whole of her conduct admirably consonant with the best tactics of feminine warfare. Vauban[1] was a fool compared to a woman determined to carry a man by storm.

Clara is now in England. She and her husband have taken a house for the season, very nearly opposite to us, in this Terrace. To-day she is going up to Liverpool, then on to Man-

---

[1] A celebrated French engineer and marshal, 1633–1707.

chester, to sing at some concerts; and she returns shortly to resume her engagements at Exeter Hall. She gave me to dwell in the seventh heaven lately, by her singing of Haydn's "Creation." That divine purity of voice of hers shows to peculiar advantage in such sublime subjects. Great as she is in operatic music, I even prefer her in sacred music. I have lately had the pleasure of enjoying my sister Emma's society for a short period. She stayed with me here, on her way from Devonshire, where she has been staying with an aunt who is very fond of her. She has obtained a very honourable appointment at Genoa, to be English professor in a college there, lately established by several influential ladies, at the head of whom is the Queen of Sardinia. The object of the institution is chiefly, I understand, to establish a more liberal system of education for young ladies than has hitherto been obtained in Italy — a most laudable view; but as yet I believe it is entertained somewhat *sub rosa*. Emma and I, as you may suppose, had " mony a crack thegether " anent a certain kind Enthusiast. . . .

When I tell you that one of the Shakespearean knacks which you forbid my sending you out by my brother's clerk in May is a copy I got Emma to make me for you of Havell's sketch of your daughter-in-love as Mrs. Quickly, I think you won't repeat your veto, will you? It is a precise representation of the dress I wore on that — to me — memorable occasion; I cannot say so much of the general likeness. The figure gives you the idea of a taller woman than your little M. C. C.; and the features are too good for hers, though Alf says that it lacks the "Novello laughing eyes." I thank you warmly for those delightful portraits. When Charles was in Edinburgh he was told that the Rev. Sydney Smith, on being introduced to Daniel Webster, gazed upon him intently for some time, and then turned to a by-stander and said: "It's like looking at a cathedral!" Charles also told me, while we were turning to the portrait of Washington Irving, that Mrs. Shelley had once said to him that she found W. I. a most delightful person. The face certainly gives you the idea of a very lovable man.

I do *not* know the state of the funds for the purchase of the house at Stratford-on-Avon; but I will endeavour to ascertain before I next write to my Enthusiast. . . .

Affectionately,

MARY COWDEN CLARKE.

Note from Charles Cowden Clarke.

MY DEAR SIR, — I have only to say that my Molly is anything but a beauty, but the "Quickly portrait" of her is not a flattering likeness. Some are born lovely, some achieve loveliness, and some have loveliness thrust upon them. The two first qualities are exemplified in your " daughter-in-love "; not so the last, as regards the portrait in question.

With kind regards to Mrs. Balmanno,

Yours most truly,

C. COWDEN CLARKE.

———

MAY 14, 1852,

27 PORCHESTER TERRACE, BAYSWATER.

MY DEAR FATHER-IN-LOVE :

L AST year a musical friend asked Alf to obtain all the Novello signatures in one page of his album; so I took the opportunity when we were in Nice of having a duplicate page written, thinking my Enthusiast might like to have it. . . .

Clara has been chatting with me, since I wrote the above. She was at the Palace last night, having been honoured by a command from Her Majesty to sing to her on her birthday. Clara knew I should be interested to hear " all how and about it," so came over to tell me the particulars of her Royal visit. It seems the Queen was most gracious, and even kind, — came to the pianoforte, and stood talking to Clara and paying her all manner of amiable

10 [145]

compliments upon the beauty of her voice, etc., etc. It was extremely gratifying altogether.

Yesterday I had the pleasure of receiving your delightful account of the Shakespeare celebration extracted from the newspaper, and the newspaper itself. Many thanks, my dear sir, and for the very elegant incidental notice of your daughter-in-love. Charles and I were both struck with the judicious terms in which it was brought in. The festival must have been a most charming one; and I think must have enchanted Mr. Burton. I thought his grave and dignified mode of receiving the honours paid him was in the best taste. I had a second letter from Mr. Allibone last week, in which he "still harps upon my daughter," or, in other words, upon my offspring the Concordance, and my method of compilation. I have answered him in full, as well as I could, explaining the plan I pursued. He seems to be a most courteous gentleman, and facetious withal. But it is high time to conclude my long gossip; so, with kindest love to my dear Mrs. Balmanno, and cordial remembrances from my men-folk to her and yourself, believe me to be

Your loving

MARY COWDEN CLARKE.

JULY 12, 1852,
27 PORCHESTER TERRACE, BAYSWATER.

MY DEAR FATHER-IN-LOVE:

YOUR very kind letter of the 27th June is just come to hand, and makes me reproach myself with having so long delayed writing to you. But I have been very closely at work, writing one book, writing another, besides occasional magazine articles, so that I have denied myself the indulgence of letter-writing almost entirely, until I fear I must have made some of my friends think me ungrateful. . . .

You affectionately notice your daughter-in-love's change of residence, and ask if Angel William still hangs at her bedside. Assuredly he does, the guardian angel to be the first face — together with my mother's, which hangs close by him — to greet my waking eyes. Did I tell you that underneath his portrait I have written his own words: "A rarer spirit never did steer humanity."[1] . . .

Your story of Miss Lucy Henry of Virginia is most lively and interesting; many thanks to you for it. I also very much enjoyed your graphic account of your ride over to Bloomingdale; and your resolve to take your wife and boys

---

[1] "Antony and Cleopatra," Act V, Scene I.

afterwards there with you charmed me especially. How pleasantly you describe the American "frolic." It must indeed be a passing
delectable kind of a holiday. It was just like
your good taste to think of having a "mul-
berry frolic" in honour of Shakespeare; the very
sort of feast to do him appropriate honour
— hearty, open-air, genuine enjoyment. Your
description of the newly invented caloric engine
afforded the Trihominate great gratification.
They jointly thank you by the pen of their least
worthy member for the kind pains you took to
tell them the narrative. I was particularly delighted with your description of your garden
and your lovely flowers; of your contrivances
for training those superb convolvulus blossoms,
well called morning-glories. We have some —
I know not whether of precisely the same kind,
but very like what you depict — at Nice, which
glow in rich profusion just at the season we are
there; also, of your glorious roses, my favourite
of all flowers. What a gorgeous sight must be
the profusion in your charming rose-embowered
cottage!

You ask what Boston Journal it was that Mr.
Dennet applied to me to write for. I think it
was called "The Boston Evening Journal," but
I am not quite sure; for the copy of the paper

that contained the reprint of one of my contributions was for that reason sent away, that the editor of the London one from which it was taken might see that he was honoured by quotation in America. I have not heard since from the Boston editor; so it is probable that my terms do not suit the proprietors. I saw a Boston gentleman a short time since; he accompanied Mr. Dennet on a morning call which that gentleman and his wife and two of his pretty little golden-haired children favoured us with. The Boston gentleman's name was Mr. Fields. I have heard him spoken of as the Moxon of Boston. He was very courteous, and spoke in most obliging terms of your daughter-in-love's estimation in America. He had been in Italy this spring, and was extremely polite and conversational.

Madame Anita George, and Mr. Kimball of New York, paid a visit here this summer. She is very pretty and lively mannered. I have to thank you for a copy of the New York Herald, containing that extraordinary account of Judge Edmonds's visions, etc. Miraculous! Also one containing an account of Mrs. Sinclair's acting; and a copy of the New York Tribune, with a speech of Mr. Webster's. . . .

I shut myself up in my den all day long, and

only issue out to take my daily health-walk in the Park, to meet my men-folk. Charles and I are up at five o'clock, take a shower-bath, and then repair to the den to work together till breakfast time. So hard do we work just now, that sometimes of an evening he gets through a second day's labour here, after having done a fair day's clerkifying at Dean Street; and you would applaud my self-denial if you knew how many treats of music I have given up this season, real temptations to me, since Clara has been singing here. She is engaged at the Provincial Festivals this autumn, and then goes straight to Madrid, they having secured her as their prima donna during their opera season till next spring. . . .

You rightly guess, my dear Enthusiast, that I certainly do not like you the worse for hearing that you are pronounced to be so like my beloved Charles. "A striking resemblance," you say. Yes, he is very lively and sprightly in his demeanour, and has a quaint style of saying vehement things in a most peculiar way. Of course you have received the numbers already out of "Bleak House." Not only I, but my mother and two of my sisters agree with me, in thinking the sketch of Mr. Boythorne remarkably like our Charles. It is an odd coincidence, for Mr. Dickens has seen so little of him[1] that it is quite impossible it can have been copied from his manner. But that vivacity of speech, that impetuosity and exaggeration in the delivery of his sentiments, with extreme heartiness and humour mingled, is strikingly like. Your friendly counsels to Mr. Plank will be invaluable to him; pray accept my cordial thanks for your goodness.

Do you know, your vegetable diet plan does not altogether please me; I fear it may not be sufficient support. Remember what our wise friend Bacon says about inclining toward "the more benign extreme," the "full eating rather than fasting;" and how he bids "beware of sudden change in any great point of diet." The conclusion of your letter lies before me, and my eyes seized upon those most loving fatherly words, "Heaven bless you, darling." From my heart of hearts I thank you for them, and entreat you to believe me

Your affectionate
MARY COWDEN CLARKE.

---

[1] As the reader doubtless remembers, Dickens drew the character from that of Walter Savage Landor.

Aug. 3, 1852,
27 Porchester Terrace, Bayswater.

My dear Father-in-love:

YOUR letter dated July 17 reached me last evening, and filled me with concern for the serious accident that occurred to you. Thank God no bones were broken, and that no permanent results befell. No doubt this is greatly owing to the temperate habits you speak of, for though I preached up generous living in my last, yet I have no doubt, care and regularity in diet tend greatly to render casualties to the frame of comparatively little consequence. Your thinking of your daughter-in-love at that particular crisis went to my heart of hearts; for well do I know by experience that, at such supreme moments, the thought of those we most intensely love is the one which springs unbidden into the soul, and fills it.

What a darling woman your Mary must be to have quietly put that portrait where it would meet your eyes on waking! My mother and I agree she must be a most lovable being, to foster as she does your partiality for your chosen favourite. Tell her, if she and I could have some quiet moments together, we would compare notes on the policy, the wisdom, of cultivating our husband's fancy for another woman whom he can esteem and love. Charles has one or two of these pleasant feminine idols, and I am never prouder or happier than when any proof occurs of his and their mutual liking. I am convinced that this kind of friendship is among the things best tending to the perfectioning of men. It appeals to their gentlest and most generous feelings, it calls forth their kindliest sentiments, and excites their worthiest ambitions. I am sure my dear Mrs. Balmanno agrees with me; for you yourself have been good enough to own much that confirms this, and my Charles has frequently confessed that nothing has given him a more honourable pride than the attachment that subsists toward him from his female friends.

You are very kind to be so well pleased with the trifles I had the pleasure of sending, and as kind to be candid in pointing out what disappointed you. I can readily imagine that the sight of her you are accustomed to exalt in your idea, in that theatrical dress, was at first a kind of disappointment. The fact is, it is less a portrait of M. C. C. than an exact representation of her costume as Mrs. Quickly. I think I told you so. I prepared you for its being rather a picture of the dress worn on that occasion than a likeness of face or figure. It is singular, your

fancying me in a "robe of darkest grain," for I
almost invariably wear black. I have hardly
ever worn anything else since the year I lost
my brother Edward.

You are quite right in the inference you draw
from the expression in my father's eye and mouth,
that he can be a humourist. He was at one time
one of the most inveterate punsters you ever
knew. He and Leigh Hunt used to pun against
each other, which could make the worst — and
consequently the best — puns, during the evening. . . .

You ask if you may not add the line you
speak of to those at the back of Mistress
Quickly's picture. Assuredly; and if you refer
to the bill of the amateur performance which
I once sent you, you will state precisely the
object of those performances.

I do not wonder, my dear sir, that Mr. Allibone should not have mentioned to you my
letters to him; he did not think it worth while,
as they were mere notes of reply to his obliging
letters. The fact is, I am unable to extend my
correspondence, for my time is already so much
occupied in writing that I am compelled to give
up a great deal of my letter-writing, and certainly
to be careful of not adding more to my list of
correspondents than I can avoid.

And now, my dear sir, let me thank you very, very heartily for the gift of the black walnut box and its contents, which reached me quite safely last Saturday. . . . You depreciate these gifts, but one of the points for which you abuse them is the very one that enhances their welcomeness to us: you say they are "ver' cheap, ver' cheap!" Now, that is one of the charms of a present between friends. Its cost should form none of its merits. Something that shall be in constant use, and at the same time inexpensive, is the beau ideal of a keepsake from one intimate friend to another. . . . Emma tells me in her last letter (from which I have cut out the enclosed vignette, that you may see the spot she now resides in; if you remember, there is a charming description of this very house in Dickens's "Pictures of Italy") that your cedar tub is immensely admired there — for she took it with her.

The very day my last letter was posted to you, I received a book from Mr. White — a superb book — "Truths Illustrated by Great Authors." A daughter may take the liberty of telling her father-in-love that she does not like him to make such costly presents. And believe her, when she says that she much rather accepts a trifle of no money value. The account of your little bird, in the one to the former lady, charmed me particularly. In the one to the latter, I perceive you put the question, Who was Campaspe? You will have doubtless remembered ere this that she was one of Alexander the Great's mistresses, with whom Apelles the painter became enamoured. My acquaintance with her was through that exquisite little song quoted in the dear old "Indicator" of Leigh Hunt:

> "Cupid and my Campaspe played
> At cards for kisses; Cupid paid," etc.

By the way, did you know that my mother was the godmother of the "Indicator"? She suggested its name, and Leigh Hunt adopted it, and the passage as a motto [1] which she had pointed out as affording ground for a good title.

You grieve me, my dear sir, by offering any excuse for sending letters to post and forward. Surely you must feel that any service we can render you is a gratification conferred upon us, —you, who have done, and are continually doing, so many kindnesses on our behalf! You ask me in that letter of July 8th whether the Trihominate are Whigs or Tories. Neither, my dear sir; staunch Liberals, all three!

---

[1] "A dram of sweet is worth a pound of sour." — *Spenser*.

I am so rejoiced that your letters and box arrived in time for me to acknowledge their safe receipt before we left England. Alf talks of some day next week for our departure for Nice. I shall hope to find, on my return home, a letter from my kind Enthusiast. . . .

MARY COWDEN CLARKE.

ROBERT BALMANNO, ESQ.

Affectionate remembrances to Mrs. Balmanno.

DEC. 13, 1852,
27 PORCHESTER TERRACE, BAYSWATER.

MY DEAR ENTHUSIAST:

I HAD the pleasure of receiving your charming letter of Nov. 25th and 26th, last Saturday. I was first beginning to devour it to myself, but my men-folk twitting me with my selfishness, and laughingly hinting that there were of course secrets in it from my Enthusiast, that I wished first to read quietly, I indulged them; and, the Trihominate drawing cosily around the fire, we all three enjoyed your most pleasant letter aloud. . . .

How very good of you, my dear sir, to send me the cast and the inkstand you mention; I shall prize them both most dearly. Alf has promised me to take means for their being

fetched from the docks in the manner you
kindly designate. Don't you depreciate, as you
are so fond of doing, your own handiwork. I
have no doubt the case you speak of as so
"bunglingly done" is very nicely arranged. I
have a particular fancy for anything that bears
the mark of home-work. The very want of finish,
which bespeaks the absence of mere mechanical
skill belonging to the regular workman's work,
is to me a charm. It proclaims that some friend
has been kind enough to prefer trying to please
himself, to buying a shop-perfectioned article.
That's why I dote on my three lamp-shades;
that's why the blue and gold covers of the ink-
stands I took to Italy were so much admired;
they show that a friend's hand has been employed
to produce something that shall gratify those he
loves. There's a grace in amateur work high
above professional work. My mother used to
prefer my cap-making to any Regent Street mil-
liner's, and I almost grudge Sabilla her having
succeeded to my post of cap-maker to "Niobe."
Charles fancies my waistcoat-stitching in preference to a tailor's, and generally honours a silk or
velvet vest of my fashioning when he lectures.
I never dream of buying a fashionable porte-
monnaie while my sisters are so kind as to fur-
nish me with purses of their own knitting; and

am prouder than I could be of any shop embroidery of a certain lovely apron which Niobe flowered over for me with rosebuds and leaves in natural colours upon black satin. There is a pleasant perpetual reminder of sentiment about home-work. I flattered myself I was doing better homage to your kind gift of those portraits of honoured Daniel Webster, of Washington Irving, of Bryant, and of Cooper, by getting glasses for them, and simply fashioning a certain plain framing of my own, with my own hands, for our book-room, than if I had sent them to a carver and gilder's to be properly mounted and framed. I think I know enough of your sentiment in such matters, my dear Enthusiast, to feel sure that you will agree with me in these whims of fancy.

You are very good to have thought of sending me some account of Mr. Thackeray's lectures and reception. I thank you for the very interesting papers you sent me respecting the lamented Daniel Webster. It was exactly the act of an affectionately considerate father-in-love, to put that mourning mark round the exterior of the paper, received Nov. 3rd, containing the account of the great man's sudden death. It prepared [me for] a shock, which as it was, was great. I read with much interest the eulogium on the deceased contained in the second paper, which arrived at the close of last month. You may imagine with what sad yet reverential feelings I sat in my chair the next time after receiving the fatal news, and with how much mournful gratification I looked again at the words traced by his pen, and contemplated the half eagle that had passed through his hands. They have now acquired a sacred interest in my eyes.

I felt certain that you would enjoy the account of our charming Italian holiday. That is quite an Enthusiast's exclamation: "Florence! that city of my soul!" . . . I knew, too, you would be gratified with the notion of finding our Niobe in her namesake's hall. With regard to your question respecting the size of the Tribuna,[1] according to the best of all our recollections, there was of course considerable discrepancy of evidence on the spur of the moment, even from the assembled members of the Trihominate alone. I said about twenty or twenty-four feet; Charles said twenty-four or twenty-five feet; Alf said it must be much nearer forty feet in diameter.[2] It is, as you correctly state, of octagonal form, and very lofty in proportion to its length and breadth. It is dome-like at the top; and the crimson ground of the whole is there inlaid with

---

[1] Uffizzi Palace.

[2] The Tribuna is about thirty-eight feet in diameter.

pearly scollop shells. In the first place, its
great height tends to make it seem smaller than
it is; and in the next place, it is a side room into
which you turn from an immensely long and wide
gallery, — the principal one, — which extends
round the quadrangle of the piazza beneath,
where are ranged colossal statues of Florence's
illustrious men. You may judge that the Tribuna
must be of greater space than is conveyed by
the impression it produces upon the spectator
on first entering, when I tell you, that besides
the Venus, the "goddess of your idolatry," it
contains four other pieces of sculpture: the
"Lottatori," "The Dancing Faun," the "Slave
overhearing the Conspiracy," and the "Apollo."
Your friend is under a mistake respecting the
glass case; at least, the Venus does not stand
beneath one now. It is, however, surrounded
by a brass railing to protect it from the too
near approach of the spectators: this contains
four other pieces of sculpture. There are also
several large damask-covered armchairs; and I
remember that when Niobe used to sit in one of
these, and we all standing about her, there was
space between our party and the pedestals, and
that other parties were constantly passing and
repassing, visitors and artists; and that of the
latter, there were more than one copying, so that

considerable space was occupied by their easels, stools, etc. This shows that Alf's estimate must be nearest to being correct; but I shall not fail to collect other evidence by the time I write to you again.

The pictures I think are all in the same places which they seem to have occupied in this room when Hazlitt visited it. You remember his delightful account of it, in his "Notes of a Journey"? Now I marvel at his omitting to especially eulogize one picture there, which enchants me: it is Guercino's Sibyl. It is a most exquisite piece of art, to my thinking. The face is a perfect ideal of rapt and inspired thought, high intelligence, and womanly beauty. Guercino is one of my idols; he has so much intellectual refinement, as well as art-excellence. Do you recollect the expression of that "St. Cecilia" of his, in our Dulwich Gallery? It is a consummate representation of a face in the act of listening. The expression is absolutely perfect; and the hands are placed on the organ keys with no less grace and appropriateness than they are charmingly painted. There is a wonderful picture of this master in one of the palaces at Genoa. It is a dying Cleopatra. It may not be precisely "the serpent of old Nile," but it is a glorious painting of a beautiful female

form, extended upon a rich background of dark
velvet drapery.   Titian himself, I think, never
excelled the colouring of the flesh; and the
feminine charm of the face and attitude, to my
taste, greatly surpass his achievements in that
particular.   I of course thought deeply of dear
Hazlitt, when I saw some of the chefs d'œuvre
of this latter artist, whom he so idolized.   The
" Ippolito dei Medici," and the portrait known
as the " Bella di Tiziano," both in the Pitti
Palace at Florence, are fully worthy even of the
exalted praise he lavished upon them.   But I
think, altogether — though it is difficult to pick
out the favourite among so many choice beauties
— my greatest charmer of all the pictures in the
Palazzo Pitti was Guido's " Cleopatra."   It is loveliness itself.   I used to sit by the hour together
opposite to that picture, luxuriating in the two
several embodiments of that scene by Guido and
by our Willie Shakespeare, both perfect in their
respective art-realizations, yet each so different.
In the one the coldish drapery, the few pearls
among the hair, the simple basket of figs, — her
luxuriance of personal beauty the sole rich point
in the picture; in the other the royal tires, the
dramatic fitness in the contrast of the voluptuous
imperial woman with the earthy grinning boor,
the poisonous asp, the attendant woman, all the

pomp and circumstance of death invoked by regal feminine will.

Yes, my dear sir, you did tell me before that your other correspondent had not mentioned the query respecting Campaspe, although M. C. C. had. . . .

MARY COWDEN CLARKE.

Kindest compliments and regards to Mrs. Balmanno.

———

JAN. 17, 1853,
27 PORCHESTER TERRACE, BAYSWATER.

MY DEAR FATHER-IN-LOVE:

I SIT down to have a gossip with you, not because I have anything particular to say, — a woman, you know, can always find something to say, though there should be nothing to say, — but because this blustering season, when I have been perpetually hearing "the rain and wind beat dark December,"[1] my thoughts naturally recur to the poor "freighting souls" in the ships at sea on the broad Atlantic, and then take placid refuge with one who dwells on " the other." And then I am seized with a longing to chat with him and tell him that with the New Year his daughter-in-love breathed a fervent prayer for his seeing many happy ones, and

———

[1] "Cymbeline," Act III, Scene III.

trusted that the past one had dealt as gently and kindly with him as with her, which (on reviewing its occurrences and events) she owned it had done, in all gratitude and thanksgiving. And she hoped he felt sure that she had not forgotten his honoured name, in her kind wishes on behalf of all those she loved, at home and abroad, at the period of Christmas, "when the bird of dawning singeth all night long,"[1] and affectionate thoughts are rife, "so hallowed and so gracious is the time."[2] Do you not think some of these wakeful nights (provided illness or anxiety has no share in their sleeplessness) when, as old Chaucer hath it, "I had ne sicknesse ne disease," are very pleasant? So many placid thoughts of those we love, so many solemn yet peaceful and hopeful aspirations for them, have place in our hearts, that the hours pass anything but drearily. If I am much excited during the daytime with any matter I have in hand, I am apt to wake soon after my first hour's sleep, and lie dreaming, with my eyes closed but with their senses open. This kind of somnambulism, where the brain alone is walking, the faculties only in activity, is far from disagreeable to my taste. Don't you agree with me?

[1] "Hamlet," Act I, Scene I.
[2] *Ibid.*

I have to thank you for a paper containing an account of St. Andrew's celebration and Mrs. Balmanno's song; they arrived Dec. 20. Also for the lovely face of " Niobe's Daughter," and the delightful inkstand. This latter is such a favourite with us, that Charles declares it to be his — all my possessions being his — and that he will allow me to use it. Seeing that whenever he writes I write, while he is at home this arrangement suits charmingly. How very beautiful is that face of the " Niobe's Daughter," — the expression not suffered to mar the natural loveliness. Those old sculptors had marvellous witchery. Do you remember what Jean Richter finally said on first seeing the treasures of Greek sculpture? — " The repose of perfection, not of weariness, looks from their eyes, and rests upon their lips. Whenever in future I write of great or beautiful objects, these gods will appear before me and reveal to me the laws of beauty." That life of Jean Paul — partly an autobiography — I was very much delighted with, when I read it some time since. I was told that it was translated and compiled by an American lady. Do you know her name?

Do you see the " Household Words "? I now and then see a number, the Christmas numbers, for instance; and I have been charmed with some verse by a young poet, which I met with there. I own I took the "Host's Story" to be by dear Leigh Hunt. "I think we do know the sweet Roman hand,"[1] but it seems I was mistaken, and that it was by the same which penned the "Idyl" in the previous year's Christmas number — very charming also. The "Masque of the New Year," likewise, quite in the genuine taste and sweet versification of Leigh Hunt's school. I wish you would read them, particularly the "Host's Story," and tell me if you don't think the narrative (like an Arabian tale, a Sinbad adventure put into ballad rhyme), the turn of thought, the easy yet terse expression, all wonderfully in his style. I own myself quite smitten with this young poet's verse. It is so delicious nowadays to meet with smooth, clear, understandable, true poetry. In this age of crabbed obscurity and far-fetched, incomprehensible mysticism under the name of fine writing, it is perfectly refreshing to come upon such a wholesome spring of poesy as the one in question.

I am happy to tell you that our letters from Nice, Genoa, and Madrid continue to bring us welcome news of the family health. Dear Niobe and I interchange rivalries and amicable competitions, as Sir Hugh Evans might call them,

---

[1] "Twelfth Night," Act III, Scene IV.

respecting the relative success of our several
Christmas puddings. Mine was a perfect achievement (between you and me, credit is entirely due
to my worthy Abigail and cook, Moss, who takes
pride in making her Christmas pudding equal
the good old times when Mrs. Novello — always
" missus " still with her, I 'm only Mrs. Clarke —
was regnant in our little household), and pronounced by the Trihominate, in solemn council,
to be matchless. My mother's — her *bonne* and
cook is only a foreigner, poor thing, so how can
she expect to make an A 1 English dish ? — was
a comparative failure. This was owned ; but my
mother intends, for the honour of England, to
have another trial. There are one or two friends
of my mother's in Nice who have entered into
this national jest, all of them having a slice of
her pudding, and sitting or eating in judgment
upon it. One of them, an English lady — an
old pupil of my father's, now married to an
Italian, and settled in Nice — affects to enter
the list of contest with her, and make a Christmas pudding in rivalry, competing for the palm.
I hear that another of the little circle, the Marchese di Negro, famed for his improvisatore
powers, has composed a poem on the occasion
of Niobe's pudding-ordeal. This darling old
gentleman, who is a great favourite with my

Sabilla, and upwards of eighty years of age, has enchanted my mother by his playful entering into a gay jest with all the vivacity and spirit of youth. In writing me an account of it, she took occasion to say how charming it was to see men of intellect, in advanced life, keep up the grace and animation and kindly playfulness and interest in cheerful subjects, that their dear old Marchese and my kind Enthusiast make a point of doing. She observed how truly wise and philosophical they showed themselves, preserving youth amidst advancing years by their liveliness and good taste. I should perhaps ask your forgiveness for this long pudding-story; but I told you at the outset of my letter that I was going to gossip and merely scribbled down anything that came into my head.

While I am on whimsical topics, let me tell you a whim I detected your M. C. C. in the other day. I have a way of keeping my papers sorted in little supplementary portfolios of any odd paper I can lay hold of. I could have plenty of new smooth sheets from dear old Alf, by only asking for them, from Dean Street. But I like such scraps as I 've any pleasant association with; and I could n't help smiling to myself — as I hope you 'll do when you read this — to find how many of these scraps were of a cer-

tain buff paper — delightfully tough of texture,
yet smooth and glossy of surface — which had
come to me at various times round divers
American packets. I like these folios thus
much better than if they had been fresh, un-
used pieces. . . .

How charmingly the "Bleak House" goes
on, does n't it? By the by, you remember, of
course, the immortal Mrs. Crackit's Christmas-
pudding anxieties in the "Christmas Carol,"
apropos of my story detailed above. Your
Royal Douglas is to appear in Royal Presence
this week. I hear that next Friday his new
comedy is to be played for the first time in the
Rubens Room at Windsor, for the Queen's
Palace Theatricals. This is a delightful and
most due honour, is it not? Charles has been
lecturing down at Sherborne this last week, at
the Institution there, which was opened by an
admirable speech — which you may probably
have seen reported in the papers at that time —
in honour of literature and literary institutions,
by its President, Mr. Macready, who had recently
purchased an estate in that neighbourhood, and
settled there on his retirement from the stage.
He has lately suffered severe domestic bereave-
ments, having lost his wife, and a grown daughter, to whom he was said to be passionately

attached. When Charles arrived he found a most elegant letter from Mr. Macready, regretting that he could not receive him, as he could have wished, at his own house, and stating his sad condition as the reason. Both Charles and I were, as you may imagine, greatly touched and gratified by this kind courtesy, especially under the circumstances. But on the few occasions on which I have had intercourse with Mr. Macready, I have uniformly found him to be in his private courtesy what you might have expected from his public career; wherein he maintained the true honour and dignity of his profession, and sedulously devoted himself to the promotion of the best interests of his art, and the highest illustration and representation of our Idol's creations. Not one of his least worthy deeds, while he was manager, was his care in seeing that his theatre was dedicated as strictly as possible to its legitimate purpose; and so assiduously did he labour and preserve it from the contamination of visitors who did not come solely to enjoy the play, that I can assert from my own experience it was scarcely more difficult for a lady to go to Drury Lane Theatre while he was controller there than to enter her own drawing-room alone. I remember once if not twice, Charles and I met there by appointment, in the particular box we always took seats in, when his engagements prevented his accompanying me at first into the house. And certainly during no other season than that do I remember such a thing being within the range of possibility for a woman to do. That season we went very, very often, both on account of the circumstance I refer to, and because Mr. Macready very generously paid us the compliment of putting down both our names on the free list, which you may imagine was an honour and privilege of which your daughter-in-love was not a little proud. To tell you a secret, she was so proud of it, her head was so turned by it, that the first time she signed her name in the great book at the free entrance, she was so giddy with her exaltation she hurried away forgetting to take her pass-check. You may imagine how Charles laughed at me. And how I laughed at myself, when I got to the head of the great staircase and was asked for it, and we had to go back ignominiously and fetch it of poor old Mr. Massingham, who I think was then still the occupant of that charmed little portal!

What a long "pribbles and prabbles" have I scrawled to you, all about nonsense and nothingness!

I tell Niobe sometimes that I often find myself seized with a longing to sit at her feet and
lay my head in her lap and chat rubbish by the
hour, as I used to do in the old happy times,
when I had nothing to do but seek her in the
next room, after a hard day's work in my own
den. Think of me always, dear kind friend, as
Your gratefully affectionate

M. C. C.

FEB. 17, 1853,
27 PORCHESTER TERRACE, BAYSWATER.

MY DEAR FATHER-IN-LOVE :

LAST Monday being set apart in the calen-
dar as especially propitious to amicable
correspondence, and moreover, bringing with it
an American post, I had half a hope that it
might have brought me a valentine from my
American Enthusiast. So long as it is not
indisposition that prevents his writing, I am
content to abide his own time, — indisposition
of body, I mean, for I know his affection is
always well enough disposed toward honoured
M. C. C.

I have to thank you, my dear sir, for a copy
of a paper, the " New York Herald," containing
an account of the Ericsson caloric ship, directed
pleasantly and conjointly to the Trihominate

[173]

and J. A. N. We were excessively interested with the details; and you may be sure your daughter-in-love's eyes filled sympathetically at that description of the inventor's emotion on seeing the device upon the vessel. I could well understand that it was not merely pride and gratified vanity which called forth his manly tears; but the inward sense of triumph and joy, to behold before him the actual proof that the idea which had so long been a truth to himself was now become a visible truth to his fellow-men, and that there it was, a palpably embodied fact, in the eyes of the whole world. Your kind thought in sending the paper enabled me not to appear quite a dunce upon the subject, when, a few days after, chance brought me next to a gentleman at a dinner-table who was full of the Ericsson ship marvels. . . .

Do you ever take lunch with you to the Custom House? I always beg my Charles to take a sandwich with him to Dean Street, and I attribute somewhat of the very regular health which, thank God, he enjoys to this practice. I have made him two little fold-up cases, so that they may be washed and kept perfectly fresh and fair, for the purpose of carrying what our friend Dugal Dalgetty[1] calls his "provant." Now it

---

[1] "Legend of Montrose," by Walter Scott.

would give me one of my peculiar fanciful pleasures if my dear father-in-love would let me make him two such sandwich cases. It would be a delight to me to know that some of his M. C. C.'s needlework accompanied him daily, to and from his own house. It would be a whim just after your daughter-in-love's own heart, if you would allow me to imagine that you also would take some gratification in this. Will you?

We have had some snow at last; we began to fancy that we were to pass through winter without having a touch of his white wand. Our accounts from Nice continue excellent, thank God! They also have had snow on the mountains to their north, but scarcely near them. The grand old fellow which towers at the end of the valley there, and forms the background to my dear mother's view from her little drawing-room window, was capped with white lately, but his hood did not spread into a mantle.

I am happy to say the news from Genoa is better. Clara's little Portia — who, with her young sister Valeria is at the college there, with their Aunt Emma — is recovering. The darling child is decidedly delicate. Clara herself, I am thankful to say, continues well and prosperous, at Madrid with her husband. . . .

MARY COWDEN CLARKE.

Trihominate best regards to you and Mrs. Balmanno. Alf talks of writing to you soon about the change in his Broadway appointments.

Mar. 22, 1853,
27 Porchester Terrace, Bayswater.

My dear Father-in-love:

THIS morning's post has just brought me your delightful letter dated Mar. 7th, together with the New York paper of the 8th. But I have also to acknowledge two other charming letters. . . . The first of these two latter ones grieved me deeply with its news of your fearful accident (though, thank God, it was no worse, and left no more lasting effects), and also of the terrible cough from which you have been suffering. Cough, and bronchitis, and "grippe"—which is a continental word for that affection of the throat which is frequently so fatal—have been awfully prevalent, both here and abroad, this last winter season. Our dear Niobe writes us word of the ravages it has made at Nice; though, thank Heaven, she and Sybil and my father and Emma and the chicks at Genoa, as well as Clara and her husband at Madrid, have escaped. Clara mentions that the

[176]

Madrid people are cruelly subject to pulmonary affections. It is intensely cold there in winter; though so extremely hot in summer.

I do not wonder at your enthusiasm respecting the volume of Mr. Collier's containing those emendations. Charles, who has been going carefully through them, has been greatly struck with most of them. You may judge how excessively busy I must have been, and am, when I tell you that I have not yet found time to read the volume. Is not that a fine solution of the difficulty with regard to the word "blanket" in Lady Macbeth's speech? — "Nor Heaven peep through the *blankness* of the dark," etc.[1] Is it not a fine, true, poetical image? And is it not a most probable printer's error, the old double *s* being so queerly made, occasionally?

The daily and nightly gratitude and thanksgiving which you allude to in your letter of Mar. 8th thrilled sympathetically to my heart. . . .

Your account of your employment and your wakeful hours perfectly corresponded with certain of your daughter-in-love's habits at those times. When I can't sleep, which, in the excitement of writing something during the day upon which I am eager, frequently occurs, I also get up and

---

[1] "Macbeth," Act I, Scene V: "Nor Heaven peep through the blanket of the dark."

12   [177]

scribble. Lately, when Charles was away, this
became so constantly the case, that I got a good
deal planned ready for the following day's work.
As you truly and admirably say, "the mind is
then clear and, as it were, young;" there is a
peculiar vividness and freshness in the ideas
at that period, and there is a great comfort in
getting them fastened down upon paper before
the stir and din of day comes to disperse or
weaken them. I must tell you that lately, on
one of these wakeful occasions, I sketched out
the whole conduct of a new story. I hope it
will one day come forth in matured substance.
Meanwhile, I expect that you will fall in love
with its heroine before she sees the light, since
her name is to be Mary Brooklyn. In the in-
terim, I need not ask you to preserve, with the
chariness of a genuine lover, her style and title.
If you should feel impelled to toast her, let it be
as "M. B.," which will seem to the uninitiated
a charming conjugal compliment and a proof
of your steadfast faith to the lady of your
allegiance.

You ask me whether my seal is one of Fassie's.
In my uncertainty which seal you allude to, I'll
send you all my Shakespeare heads, with the
several accounts of each impression. I think
the title you propose for Mrs. Balmanno's book

excellent.   I am quite longing to make acquaintance with " Compositions." . . .

The origin of my mother's settling down in
Sardinia was this.   In the winter of '47 she had
a severe attack of bronchitis, that very, very nearly
deprived us of her forever.   I begged to be allowed to sleep with her, as she fancied no one
could amuse her so well as I; and I assure you,
my dear sir, there were many hours during those
long suspenseful nights when I lay listening to
her painful breathing, that filled me with the
most terrible of all dreads.   However, thank God,
she rallied, and was spared to us.   Through the
summer of '48 she had recovered, it is true, but
she became very feeble and delicate.   Sometimes when I used to see her sitting waiting to
take her daily drive out, looking pale and drawn
and eager (she is one of the most energetic of
women, her spirit of alacrity and eagerness is
like a girl of twenty and her pulse is almost
like an infant's), with that expression which
suggests the mind being too active for the
body, I had the most keen anxiety and the
sharpest fear that the struggle must end in
the defeat of the frame.   Well, in the latter
autumn of that year, Clara and her husband
were leaving their beautiful estate at Fermo,
to make some stay in Rome, and they wrote

to persuade my mother to go and winter there with them. She consented, and kindly took Emma and Sabilla with her, for the advantage and pleasure of the holiday in Italy. When she left Craven Hill Cottage that evening to set out on her journey, as she leaned on my father's arm to walk to the garden gate toward the coach, her step was so feeble, her face so white, her air altogether so frail and fragile, that my heart melted within me, while I would not own to myself the thought that filled it with a cold terror. But her journey was slow, she had two excellent nurses with her, and the letters we received from the different stages of her progress announced her gradually better and better, stronger and stronger, as she got more and more stout. On reaching Nice, she found the climate so exquisite, that although the month was November, yet the windows of her hotel apartment were open, and gave to view a garden blooming with flowers in rich, summer-like beauty. During her sojourn at Rome, the impression of Nice remained with her; and on her return next spring she stopped there for a time. The impression was confirmed by a second acquaintance with the spot; and finally she wrote us home word that she believed that if she wished to preserve herself alive for us, she must decide upon self-exile from an English climate, and remain where she was. Thus it was concluded upon; and we have had reason to bless the decision, which although it partly banished her from us, yet still retained her in "this breathing world" to contribute to our happiness whenever we could join her. That same year my father went out to her, accompanied by us Trihominate, — he staying to reside there with her, we three returning to our work, in the hope of being one day able to fulfil her desire of having us also settled with her in her Nice nest. Meantime we "snatch a hasty joy" each autumn, and have been blessed with power each year to carry it into effect.

I thought you would be amused with the pudding-history! Unfortunately, I have not a copy of those verses, they are probably not written even; for the Marchese di Negro is famous among those celebrated for improvisatore powers. I must have expressed myself ill to give you the notion that I wrote on that American yellow paper; I used it for separating-covers, or portfolios, to my different scrawlings. Therefore, my dear father-in-love, with many thanks for your kind offer, I do not wish for the quires you offer, the sheets I get at different times from you as envelopes answering my purpose capitally and having the extra charm of association.

That is a horribly dark menace of yours which you throw out in case of my not accompanying my brother to America. But in the first place, he is not going this year, and in the next, I have so invincible a terror of sea-voyaging that I think nothing could draw me to encounter that fearful Atlantic Ocean for days and nights. Those two hours of traversing the British Channel, and two hours back, are an annual agony to me. Nothing but my beloved mother's living on one side and myself on the other could induce me ever to cross it more. My imagination tortures me all the time. " How abhorred in *your* imagination it is!"[1] Will you think me a very coward if I own this? And will you forgive and not misinterpret me (for I should feel grateful for the feeling that inspired it, though the actuality would dismay me), if I confess to you that one of the very things you tell me as an inducement would act as a deterrer, — that my reception in New York and Boston would be so flattering. You do not know what a shy, odd little fish your M. C. C. is, my dear father-in-love.

[1] " Hamlet," Act V, Scene I : " How abhorred in my imagination it is ! "

What a mad absurdity this " medium " fanaticism seems to be! I have heard of a lady here, a clever though not a sensible woman — and there is a vast difference — who is bitten with this ridiculous mania to an almost incredible pitch.

Very many thanks, my kind father-in-love, for the complete sets of the " Girlhood " engravings. I am half ashamed of my boldness in asking you for them, yet only *half* ashamed either. Let me tell you a circumstance that I know will give my Enthusiast pleasure. I was at a large party in Brook Street the other evening; our kind friends Dr. Storrar and his wife are almost the only people we allow ourselves to break through our strict resolve to forbear indulging in visiting. As I was standing by the library fire, taking coffee before going up into the drawing-room, Mr. Wallace Scott — the artist of that miniature of Charles that was presented to me, and of one of Clara's likenesses — came up to me, and presently said: " I have a young sister of fifteen years of age, who, ever since Mr. Cowden Clarke gave me a copy of your ' Girlhood Tales,' has possessed herself of it, and not allowed me the use of my own property. The fact is, she has taken a prodigious fancy to the stories, and having a talent for drawing, she has pleased herself by

[183]

making illustrations to them. I saw the sketches while they were in hand, and being willing to encourage her taste and induce her to cultivate it, I praised them, pointed out one or two matters which she might improve, costume, etc., and told her that she might complete the set and make a fair copy, and I would take them to Mrs. Cowden Clarke in her name." You may imagine, my dear father-in-love, my delight. The mere notion of seeing how a young fresh heart of fifteen would view the fancies embodied in those stories gave me exquisite gratification; but when I came to see the drawings themselves, I assure you I was enchanted. So much artistic taste, delicacy of feeling, sentiment, spirit, and beauty were to be traced in the series of illustrations. I was greatly delighted, as I think you will be, to hear of it even. Niobe was charmed.

How you transport me by telling me you take luncheon, and will carry it with you daily in my needlework! It will be like accompanying you to the office and beguiling the way with chat. When I think of walking arm in arm with you, dear father-in-love, my dream of the dark Atlantic Ocean seems to pale and lessen. And yet — to see the human inconsistency! — I would rather *not* see you! It would destroy the strange romantic charm which invests our mutual friendship; intimate though unknown,— affectionately esteeming and regarding, without one interchanged spoken word. I should not like to have it destroyed, methinks.

Yes, my dear sir, I think I can answer your query why my letters now seem to have become more welcome than ever to you: it is because we know each other more thoroughly. It is a maxim of mine that a genuine attachment strengthens with time; and that we love those we truly love the more, the more and the longer we know them. The very acquaintance with thoughts and imperfections increases liking, where the liking is genuine. I am sure that Charles and I loved each other better after we were old married folk than we did when he first asked the girl of scarcely seventeen to be his wife; and I am certain we love each other more firmly and truly after more than twenty-four years of wedlock. I think this growth of liking may not be where the liking is superficial at first; but where it is a liking founded on esteem and preference, and that inexplicable sympathy which springs from like tastes, like opinions, like sentiments, I feel convinced that liking ever grows and grows, and strengthens and strengthens. You pleased me greatly by the thought that you and your

Mary are going to enjoy the " Merry Wives " together, and intend thinking of *your* Mistress Quickly.

Charles has been gloriously received in Edinburgh during his late course of lectures there, both privately and publicly; and at a fish dinner they got up in his honour at Newhaven, the Sheriff of Mid-Lothian, who was chairman, made a very elegant speech, in which he alluded to his former acquaintance with the Mistress Quickly of the Amateur Company at the time they were there in 1840. In proposing her health — which he did after Charles's — he playfully informed the company that he knew Mrs. Cowden Clarke years before he had seen her husband, and that several agreeable passages had passed between them, and that it would be a perfect Concordance to have Mrs. C. on his right and Mr. C. on his left; yet that she being absent, he was not wholly free from a little ambition to rouse Mr. C. C.'s jealousy. When Charles replied, he told the company that he wished Mrs. C. could have been present to reply herself to the presumptuous speech they had just heard; and said it was very probable that she might have quoted to them from the play in which they had seen her: " As for my good man, he's as far from jealousy as I am from giving him cause; and that, I hope, is an immeasurable distance. And as for the *fat knight*" — pointing to the chairman — " Heaven guide him to my husband's cudgel; and the Devil guide his cudgel afterwards." You may imagine this told well. Charles's late sojourn in Edinburgh has been one continual triumph. They are a delightful audience, so appreciative and exact in judgment; and in their own houses so kind and hospitable when you are a favourite. And this makes their welcome the more valuable.

I thank you very much for the accounts of the Ericsson success; it is delightful. His speech that you quote was fine. That is always the feeling of great discoverers. A most admirable mechanical genius, Mr. Bessemer, whose centrifugal pump gained great admiration at the Exhibition of '51, told Alf the other day that it was a curious thing to him to speculate on the time when all these discoveries, which are now so important, will be superseded by others yet more ingenious.

How entrancing to have you, my dear father-in-love and Enthusiast, talk of feeling young again or reading a book you enjoy. It is glorious, this privilege of prolonged youth which is accorded to those of cultivated taste and judgment, with literary likings, and art affections, added to their home loves. Long may it be enjoyed by her kind father-in-love, prays, in all sincerity,

MARY COWDEN CLARKE.

I hardly care to add separate greetings to Mrs. Balmanno, since I write to him who is one with herself. . . .

The seal impressions, the trifle-notes, and the sandwich cases, Alf has undertaken to send by his next parcel to New York.

I was compelled to cut off this last sheet on account of postage-weight; but I leave the slip on, since you tell me your ingenious method of preserving your M. C. C.'s gossip-letters. I have every one my Enthusiast ever wrote me; but they are not so cleverly arranged. God bless him!

APRIL 20TH, 1853,
27 PORCHESTER TERRACE, BAYSWATER.

MY DEAR ENTHUSIAST:

THIS April spring weather prompts me to send greetings to my kind father-in-love, since I can't wend to him in person. I trust you are by this time quite recovered from all ill effects from your accident in the winter, and that you are preparing to enjoy spring and

summer in their genial beauty. I suppose you
will be spending the day-after-the-day-after-to-
morrow in right genial and right royal fashion,
worthy of the most genial of geniuses and most
regal of poets, whose Commemoration Day it is.

We have just had a genial addition to our
Trihominate circle in the shape of Clara's
advent. She arrived in England rather more
than a week since, from Madrid. When she got
so near within range as Paris, she and Alf held
a conversation together by means of the electric
wires. Those are something like "mediums"
if you please! Their intercommunications seem
little short of spirit-intercourse. It was odd
enough to have Alf asking Clara in Paris
whether she'd come to sing the Requiem of
Mozart on the following day, and her answering
him in London, that as she felt rather tired and
lazy after her journey from Spain, she thought
she should not! A marvellous and most delightful age we live in, dear sir, to command such
powers of transmitting our thoughts thus far and
thus promptly!

They talk of a brilliant musical season in London this year. On Saturday I went with Clara
to the Philharmonic rehearsal, where she enchanted me with those supreme tones of hers in
Meyerbeer's very dramatic song of " Robert, toi

que j'aime " from Robert le Diable. Did I ever
tell you that I once embroidered her two queer
pocket-handkerchiefs, which, by the by, she tells
me she has still? In each of three corners were
the first few bars of one of her favourite arias,
surmounted by the composer's name in flourished
Old English letters, and in the fourth corner her
own name worked across the bars of an embroidered lyre. It was eccentric, but rather pretty;
for the sake of the homage involved, most sincere, as you can well imagine. One of my sisters
sometimes playfully accuses me of having an absolute idolatry for my own family, and that I
think no talent, no virtues, no excellence of any
kind, so good as theirs. She of course exagger-
ates a little, in her humorous accusation, but I
own to rather a weakness for my family's merit.

A short time since I met with one of my art-
idols — one of the family of Novello — as I was
going to town on business in an omnibus : it
was no other than John Cramer, who of all
pianoforte players used to be my favourite. I sat
next to him, as it happened. He looked once or
twice at me, thinking that he ought to know me,
I suppose, for he had formerly seen me occasionally at my father's house; but I in my foolish-
ness could not muster courage to address him,
and tell him I was the daughter of his old friend

Vincent Novello. Oddly enough, he glanced wistfully at the little roll I held in my hand, and I could not help thinking how much he would have been interested in it, could he have known of what it consisted, being a proof of Sir John Hawkins's "History of Music." Curious coincidence, was n't it? I was watching his hand and hoping he would take off his glove, when at last he did so, to take the fare from his purse; and then I saw again that fine white hand which had so many times entranced my ears with the tones it used to bring forth from the instrument. I think I never heard such a smooth legato as his; it was absolutely perfect, and with such expression and polished beauty! I could not help remembering the anecdote I had heard of him, and his witty elegant answer to one of the modern pianists,—one who possessed marvellous power with his left hand,—who said to him one day, meeting him at a party, "I understand, Mr. Cramer, you deny my having any left hand. I hope you will allow me to play to you, and convince you to the contrary." The young man played; and then the veteran John Cramer rejoined: "I still preserve my opinion, sir. I maintain that you have no left hand, but two right hands!"

Charles has gone down to Devonshire on a

lecture tour in the West of England; and next month he is to deliver his new course at the London Institution. That is always a rather nervous affair to me. So long and so great a favourite as he has been there, it has not yet cured me of my absurd anxiety; nay, I think the oftener I hear him give a new course there, the worse I am, in solicitude that he should make no less an impression than he has always made for nearly twenty years, at that first-rank Institution. A lady once told a friend of mine, who is wife of one of the managers there: "I found out which was Mrs. Cowden Clarke among the audience by her anxious face. Directly her husband made his appearance there was no mistaking her, though I had never seen her before." *You* will understand this, my dear Enthusiast, and not laugh at your foolish daughter-in-love.

Clara has brought me such a love of a black lace mantilla from Spain — a genuine Spanish mantilla. You may fancy how proud your daughter-in-love is of it! You see I must be badly off for gossip and news when I tell you such trifles as this. . . .

With kindest remembrances to Mrs. Balmanno, believe me to be

Your affectionate
MARY COWDEN CLARKE.

MAY 19, 1853,
27 PORCHESTER TERRACE, BAYSWATER.

MY DEAR FATHER-IN-LOVE:

I HAVE just had the pleasure of receiving your delightful long letter dated 5th and 7th of May, and enclosing that interesting bill of Mr. Burton's revival of the " Merry Wives." It has quite effected another revival, having revived all my old " Mistress Quickly " feelings. Please to tell Mr. Burton, with my best compliments, that could I but conquer my awe of the Atlantic sufficiently to find myself in New York I should hope to have the pleasure of playing Mistress Quickly to his Sir John Falstaff, at his theatre. In this case, I should have to ask leave of Mrs. Hughes, who you say plays the part so well. Your account of her acting, and of your thinking of your daughter-in-love through her, enchanted me. How I should like to play the character, with you in the house! What a perfect delight it would be! And then to follow it up by fulfilling my great ambition, that of enacting Maria, in " Twelfth Night," to say nothing of Audrey, the nurse in " Romeo and Juliet " and — to descend to *not* Shakespearean characters — Mrs. Malaprop, Mrs. Heidelberg,[1] etc. To tell my

---

[1] " The Clandestine Marriage," Colman and Garrick.

13   [193]

father-in-love a little secret, acting has been always a darling weakness of his M. C. C.'s; and it would be a charming thing to indulge it in presence of my indulgent Enthusiast. What a reception he would give me! If his hands were sore with applauding her through the acting of another, what would they be then?

I am greatly obliged to you for promising to send me a copy of Mr. Putnam's capital letter; I shall be most glad to read it. The account you give me of Mrs. Balmanno's beautiful idea in illustrating each page of the Shakespeare Record book interested me extremely. It must be most lovely, and, as you say, will doubtless rather astonish the Society when presented, as you propose. They must have been highly gratified by so tasteful a work, and so elegant a compliment. No, my dear sir, I understand Mr. Wallace Scott is not a born Scotchman, but a Manchester man; although he is doubtless of a Scotch family, from the name.

You ask me what I think of your neat turn of that phrase of Willie's — "'T is the heart, 't is the heart," etc. I think it very admirable. But did you mean an extra subtle turn upon me by ending it with "Mrs. *Shallow*"? If you remember, the original is, "'T is the heart, 't is the heart, Master Page," uttered by Shallow. By the by, you should have heard the admirable manner in which Charles Dickens uttered that sentence, when he played Justice Shallow; but his playing of the part altogether was superexcellent. His delivery of that other passage which you quote also, "I have seen the time, with my long sword I would have made you four tall fellows skip like rats!" was perfect — absolutely perfect.

Your account of the Shakespeare festival was charming. I had the pleasure of reading the notice in the paper which you kindly sent me some time since, to the assembled Trihominate and Clara. She has gone to the Düsseldorf musical festival. As her husband was still detained at Nice, with the sick child, — who, however, I am happy to say is pronounced greatly better, — Alfred accompanied her. He wrote us a delightful account of the effect she produced there. She sang the "Messiah" in German, and the grand scena from Glück's "Alceste." She was formerly an immense favourite in Germany, and it seems they received her among them again with a perfect rapture of enthusiasm. Alf and she must have had a delightful time; for Gigliucci persuaded my sister Sabilla to accompany him for a holiday to Germany, where she spent a great portion

of her girlhood and acquired a great liking for
the Germans, who are a kindly people. It must
have been quite a family meeting.

Sybil has persuaded Alf to go back with her
part of the way; and he, not being able to resist the temptation of going to see Niobe, talks
of paying a flying visit to Nice before he returns.
Although I regret losing him for so long a space,
yet I am rejoiced that my mother shall have
this reward for her kind unselfishness in allowing Sabilla to leave her and inducing her to
take the holiday. Alf tells me he thought of
me there, knowing my doting for nightingales;
for they are so abundant and in such full voice at
Düsseldorf just now, that they make a perfect
chorus. The Music-room there, where the festival is held, is built adjoining a large garden in
which there are at present so many nightingales
that he says, at times, during the softer parts of
the music while the performance was going on,
the birds were to be heard, as if singing against
Clara.

You are right, my dear father-in-love: I had no
need to be nervous about Charles's course of lectures at the London Institute. He never pleased
more thoroughly. The warmth and cordiality of
his reception rejoiced my wifely heart. It is now
eighteen years ago since he first made his ap-

pearance before that audience. And sixteen seasons out of the eighteen he has been engaged there. He could not refrain from adverting with pleasurable pride to the circumstance, when he took leave of them, at the end of the course, until they should next be permitted to meet; and I assure you my heart danced to note that òn this, the sixty-fourth evening of his lecturing before them, they were as enthusiastically pleased as ever. I enclose you my syllabus — I send you my own copy, knowing you will prefer the one I used to an uncrumpled new one — that you may see what were his subjects.

You ask me if I am fond of waltzing. My dear sir, I gave up dancing the very first time that I had a glimpse that I might be growing too old for it. Some one said: "Why, Mrs. C. C., you are not dancing! Let me find you a partner." The words were enough. I remembered the time when partners offered of their own accord, and did not require to be found for me. I laughed to myself, and took the timely and most significant hint, and have never danced since. Your description of the charming young Irish lady waltzer, and of the lively dialogue between you and herself, amused me exceedingly. Pray fulfil your intention of giving the lady at whose

house you met her, Mrs. Lewis, the note of introduction. Any friend of yours must always be
welcome to me. I of course did not fail to do
as you directed with regard to enclosing and
posting the letters you forwarded from the
father of my little namesake.

With kindest remembrances to Mrs. Balmanno, believe me to be

Your affectionate friend,

M. C. C.

JULY 15, 1853,
27 PORCHESTER TERRACE, BAYSWATER.

MY DEAR ENTHUSIAST:

YOUR last most kind letter reached me on
the 11th. It bears date the 26th and
29th of June. How wonderfully rapid is the
intercommunication nowadays!

Yes, my dear father-in-love, the wicked "men-
folk" of the Trihominate do laugh at the kind
Enthusiast's affectionate sallies, but they laugh
lovingly, sympathetically, as they would do at
one of their own rhapsodies. They laugh as
a cover to secret pride and pleasure, as English-
men frequently do; for they are in truth most
pleased and proud at the partiality you evince
for their "womankind." You were very good

[198]

to take so much interest in my flourish about acting as to read it to Mr. Burton, but I honour him for his loyalty to his own favourite, Mrs. Hughes. You would have preferred yours, M. C. C., to his, had the cases been reversed; and therefore you must admire him for favouring her in the same way.

I have been enjoying a great treat lately in the matter of acting. Rachel has been over here this season; and Clara tempted me to join her and Gigliucci in a subscription for the sixteen performances. The combined delight of seeing the only tragic acting I now care for, and seeing it in company with Clara and her husband, was irresistible, and I went — a great deal of dissipation for a hermit like me. She is a glorious creature ; not like a Frenchwoman, — so full of genius and poetry. Her Phèdre is one of the grandest things I ever beheld. It makes me shake, even to think of it. I was so excited at witnessing it, that I could not recover my calm for hours after. She played several of her modern dramatic characters ; but it is in the old classic drama that I love to see her. There she has full scope for her high powers. She does some fine things, doubtless, in the modern plays; but the plays themselves are so inferior in the diction and thought, that they make one regret to see her great acting wasted upon them. One of the masterly points she has is her death scene in " Adrienne Lecouvreur." It is absolutely fearful with such a terrible truth to nature. She does a very bold thing in it : she dies with her eyes open. Yet so wonderfully does she contrive the alteration of her countenance, the change of look, the fixture of the face, the gradual rigidity of the muscles round the mouth, the ghastly expression throughout, that there is no doubt upon the spectator's mind of the moment when she expires. It is a piece of consummate art, and contrasts beautifully with the earlier scenes of the play, where she is all tenderness and brilliant fascination. But at the conclusion of the series she played Camille in Racine's " Les Horaces," and I had again the delight of seeing her in one of her genuine triumphs. The imagination, the fire, the poetic grace and refinement, the *soul* she throws into every line of this noble part prove her indeed the high tragedian. Were there nothing more than the inimitable difference of intonation with which she utters those two exclamations "O! mes frères!" and "O mon cher Curiace!" upon hearing of her brother's death, and then that of her lover, Rachel would have proved herself a mistress of her art. The regret of affection

in the one sentence and the outpouring of passionate grief in the latter are marvellously dis-
criminated. The way in which she cries out
"Éclatez mes douleurs, à quoi bon vous con-
traindre?" makes me long to see her play
Shakespeare's Constance; while her line "Rome
enfin que je haïs parce qu'elle t'honore!" and
the whole concluding scene with her brother, inspired the wish that she could play that fine un-
acted scene in Henry VIII, of Queen Catherine
with the two Cardinals. I am sure she would
play Shakespeare's Constance, Queen Catherine, Lady Macbeth, and Hermione nobly —
were she capable of mastering the English pronunciation perfectly. But I suppose that is out
of the question hoping for.

I think by this time I shall have made you
laugh at my enthusiasm. Eh? Sha'n't I? But
I don't mind. We are privileged to make each
other laugh and to laugh at each other, as much
as we like; and I own my foible for Rachel, as
you do for your honoured daughter-in-love. I
duly received your kindly sent papers containing
those interesting accounts of the Shakespeare
meeting, and the progress of the Society. May
it prosper, heartily I pray! What an exquisite
book that must be of Mrs. Balmanno's, and what
a great gift to the Society! No, my dear sir,

alas, I have not thyme from Avon's banks to send you; but should I ever revisit that hallowed spot, assuredly I shall not forget your wish.

My Charles revelled in your hearty account of your brown-bread-and-tea repast. It was the true zest of enthusiasm imparting a gusto to simplest fare. Your anecdote of those Leicestershire workingmen was delightful.

It is some time since I have seen the " Athenæum " regularly; but I shall hope to do so again shortly. In what number did that "triumphant tracing" of the emended copy of Mr. Collier which you mention appear? I quite feel with you as to the strangeness of such a being's writing producing no better spirit than the contentious one that now exists among the so-styled admirers of Shakespeare. Surely, if there be one thing more than another to be derived from his works, it is a universal spirit of toleration and gentleness.

You must know that my Charles and I have just celebrated the completion of our silver year, as the Germans call the twenty-fifth year of wedlock. It is a pleasant reflection for two human beings that they have spent a quarter of a century together happily, and with increasing esteem and affection. I should be delighted if we should be permitted to achieve our golden year — the fiftieth — under no less happy circumstances.

JULY 18TH. We hope to make our annual flight to Nice for a holiday with the dear parent-birds very soon; therefore you will be prepared not to hear from me again for some time. We expect to return to England early in October. I intended to have dispatched this letter on the same day it was commenced, last Friday; but was prevented from doing so, and therefore will post it to-morrow.

The accounts of the extreme heat in New York lately are terrible. I trust you, dear sir, have not suffered either in your own person, or through any of those you love. Here we have a great prevalence of wet weather, with gusty winds and occasional bright gleams. This absurd puppet-show at Chobham attracts crowds of fashionables, idle or interested; but the showers have a little damped the ardour — polite and military. I accompanied Gigliucci and Clara last Saturday to see the German company who are playing here just now at the St. James Theatre. Very different from Rachel's performances! I confess I was greatly disappointed, after the eulogistic accounts which had been given of them in the press last year. The play we saw was Goethe's "Faust." Emil Dev-

[203]

rient is celebrated for his impersonation of the
hero; and Dessoir is considered the first Mephis-
topheles in Germany. The former I liked in the
earlier scenes, though even then he lacked that
passionate earnestness in the midst of dissatisfac-
tion which I feel to exist. As for the latter, he
seemed to me a mere caricature — an exagger-
ated, overacted impersonation of a devil, performed *at* the audience, instead of the easy,
sneering, off-hand being, assuming the guise of
a man of the world but allowing to appear
through all the spirit of evil and diabolism.
The fact is, Goethe's work is rather a dramatic
poem than a play, and, although called a tragedy,
is not fitted for stage representation. It should
be read, rather than seen; and the imagination
can supply the requisite scenes and embodiment.
The effect, on the boards, is both clumsy and dull;
all unlike the high poetic view of human life and
its aspirations, its struggles and its baffled desires,
its strength and its weaknesses, its noblenesses
and its imperfections, in which we are both carried on and entranced while perusing the drama
in our own quiet room. They say Devrient
plays Hamlet finely, but I have no wish to see
him. I remember being greatly pleased with
his sister-in-law Madame Schrader Devrient's
playing Lady Macbeth some years ago, in

Chelard's[1] operatic version of Shakespeare's
play. In the opera, Lady Macbeth is made to
awake from her sleep-walk, and find herself be-
trayed to witnesses of her guilty wanderings.
The attitude in which Schrader stood at bay
was very fine. I see it still in my mind's eye.

What a dish of theatrical gossip this letter has
been ! . . .

MARY COWDEN CLARKE.

AUGUST 9TH, 1853,
27 PORCHESTER TERRACE, BAYSWATER.

MY DEAR ENTHUSIAST:

I KNOW not how sufficiently to thank you,
and to tell you how delighted I am with
the high honour done me by the Shakespeare
Society. I am enchanted to have received your
letter announcing it, before we leave England,
as I shall thus be able to take the charming
news to my dear mother. Only imagine how
proud and happy Niobe will be ! The Trihominate enjoyed your letter conveying the intelligence of the compliment paid to me, and the
details of your interview with Lord Ellesmere
upon the like gratifying occasion, with extreme
pleasure. Most kind of you to send us the account, knowing how it would interest us. You

---

[1] A French composer, 1789–1861.

will, I know, excuse a long letter from me this time, when I tell you that I am full of business preparatory to leaving home for Italy. I enclose this in my official letter to you as Secretary of the Shakespeare Society — since I remember your predilection for non-envelopes and paper bearing post-mark. I assure you your daughter-in-love is not a little proud at having received such distinguished honours from the two great Shakespeare Societies of the globe. Clara brought me a plume of beautiful marabou feathers from Portugal, that she had of an African merchant; perhaps had she given me a plume of peacock's feathers, they would have formed a much more appropriate wear for me in my present proud condition of mind. What do you think? If I am led into the indulgence of one of the seven deadly sins — pride — I shall have to thank you for it, my dear Enthusiast! I do thank you, not for the proud pleasure so much as for the deeper gratification attaching to the generous distinction bestowed by this honorary membership. Believe me, I am properly sensible of it, and entreat you to believe me to be

Yours, sincerely obliged,
Mary Cowden Clarke.

Robert Balmanno, Esq.

Oct. 20, 1853,
27 Porchester Terrace, Bayswater.

My dear Father-in-love:

THE Trihominate being safe in their English nest once more, I write to tell you we had a very pleasant migration, and found the parent-birds quite well, and as glad as ever to gather their chicks under their wings once more. We had the pleasure of a very full assemblage; for the best songster was there, she and her mate joining us at Nice a week before we left, on their way to Milan, where Clara is engaged at La Scala for the winter season. Sabilla was well enough, I rejoice to say, to give us all a few chirps; Alf was in good voice, and your daughter-in-love and her mate did their best, so that we more than once got up a family concert for the delectation of the parent pair. Among other things, we sang a four-part Thanksgiving, composed by my father, and which at one time of our lives, when we all lived together, his children were in the daily habit of singing together, as a grace after dinner. You may imagine with what grateful emotions we found ourselves once again permitted to perform this piece together, and before him. I think he was pleased; you may believe that dear Niobe was delighted. I can't help telling you another thing

that occurred while we were there apropos of
music. Clara happened to be singing one of
Mozart's enchanting airs, one that always goes
straight to my heart, in addition to the peculiar
effect which the tone of Clara's voice always produces upon me; and at the very time she was
drawing tears from my eyes, her youngest child
was seated on the floor near, employed in tying
her own little chubby legs together, and trying
to scramble in this fashion across the slippery,
inlaid floor. The contrast was ineffably odd;
and what with crying at the mother, and laughing at the child, I was very nearly hysterical.

We were highly entertained with the enthusiasm that prevailed in France, as we passed
through on our way to Italy, on the subject of
the Napoleon fêtes. One gentleman would not
believe that we were actually in Paris at the
time and hastened out of it without staying to
see these sublime fêtes. He described them
with an eloquence that was worthy of a loftier
theme. He expatiated on the magnificence of
the illuminations, as if they had been the starry
firmament. He extolled the exhibition on the
Champs de Mars as though it had been heaven
itself. When Alf assured him that he rather
congratulated himself than regretted not having
seen the show, as he should have then been de-

prived of the full lustre and enjoyment of this flowing description, which as perfectly painted it to his fancy as he could desire, the gentleman assured him that it was not in the power of human description, or in the power of man's imagination, to depict or conceive the majesty of the whole. — " *C'etait ravissante !* " He went off into ecstasies upon the subject of the " *Sphère d'azur* " surmounted by an eagle " *qui tenait dans son bec un* " — I, who was very sleepy, thought he said " *un âne* " — but it proved to be " *un N ;* " and then he diverged into rhapsodies about the extraordinary *aplomb* and self-possession of the Emperor and Empress, and the dignity with which they occupied their seat in the carriage with eight horses, etc., etc., etc. It was a perfect specimen of the way in which Frenchmen's minds can be absorbed and held subject by shows, fêtes, illuminations, and frippery.

My dear mother and all Nice friends desired to be most kindly remembered to you when next I should write. Greetings also from us Trihominate. I shall hope to have a letter from you soon; and trust that it will contain good accounts of your health, and that of all those you love. With best compliments and regards to Mrs. Balmanno, believe me to be   Your affectionate

MARY COWDEN CLARKE.

ROBERT BALMANNO, ESQ.

14   [209]

DEC. 8, 1853,
27 PORCHESTER TERRACE, BAYSWATER.

DEAR ENTHUSIAST:

I AM vexed to find by your letter of the
15 Nov. that you yourself have been much
vexed. If I were by your side I should venture to take the same liberty with you which my
men-folk allow me to take with them when I see
them doing anything I don't think wise for them,
namely, remonstrate. I should remonstrate with
you for increasing your vexation by enquiring into
particulars that only serve to feed your ire, and
by indulging your Scots blood with venting sun-
dry wrathful epithets against those who have
heated its current. If you discovered unpleas-
ant antecedents concerning a person of whom
you once thought better and esteemed, why
augment your own annoyance by dwelling upon
them, and collecting them? If another person
has affronted you and — what I know is worse
to your enthusiasm — slighted your idols, why
foster your irritation by calling him "a seven-
feet-high giraffe"? There! I hope I've made
you smile — nay, laugh — by quoting your own
epithet. Never mind the "darling" lady of
your acquaintance named M. C. C. and the
"gentleman whose initials are very like hers," if
taking their parts puts you into these frets and

[210]

fumes, which can't be good for you. We owe it to our master, and his divine philosophy of forbearance, not to get into vexation of spirit about his writings. Let us be worshippers, rather than partisans. Excuse me if I preach; but my men-folk have spoilt me by letting me speak out when I wish it. You know what friend Sancho, with his delicious sly impudence and quaint and shrewd sense, says — " Though a woman's counsel is n't worth much, yet he that despises it is no wiser than he should be." So, be you ruled by me, my dear father-in-love; and think more of the pleasant circumstances that an adoration of Shakespeare brings about, and less of the disagreeables. To show you how naughty and prejudiced you are, I will tell you that I lately read a Shakespearean article by that same "giraffe," as you are pleased to call him, — at least I think by the name you add it must be the gentleman, — which contained some very interesting matter. And now, forgive me for my freedom in having thus spoken out to my father-in-love, on behalf of his cultivating the pleasurable and amicable in preference to dwelling upon painful things.

I knew your kind heart would take pleasure in that account of our pleasant holiday and family meeting at Nice last time. We Trihom-

inate laughed heartily at your anecdote of Cato;
Charles says he remembers hearing of the circumstance at the time it occurred. Charles had
before made enquiry at the plaister-cast shops
for the mask of Mrs. Siddons's face of which you
speak, and could hear no tidings of such a thing
being in existence. But he wrote for further
information, to Mrs. George Combe, to whom
he had the pleasure of being introduced when
last he was lecturing in Edinburgh, and this
morning received an answer; which I at first
thought of transcribing for you, but have since
resolved to enclose, thinking you might like to
possess it as an autograph letter. You remember that she is the Cecilia Siddons in Lawrence's
drawing of that fine little and comely child's
face, among a collection lithographed by Lane,
after Lawrence, of the Kemble family. What a
lovely countenance is that of Mrs. Siddons
there! And how well it bears out the one by
Reynolds of her in the Dulwich Gallery!

I thank you for the kind interest manifested
by your mention of a lecture-trip to America as
a possibly productive scheme for Charles. We
have often thought of it; but the sea is as for-
midable an obstacle to him as to me. We both
have a horror of sea-voyaging. You will be
pleased to learn — because it pleases your

daughter-in-love — that he has just received a most gratifying invitation from the Earl of Zetland, to deliver three of his lectures to a large assembly of Lord and Lady Z.'s friends, in the great hall at Aske during the coming season, as one among the entertainments and festivities with which they are going to amuse their country neighbours, etc., during Christmas. The manner of the invitation enhances the pleasure of the circumstance itself; and you may be sure that your daughter-in-love's heart rejoices extremely.

Give my loving thanks to your dear wife for her kind message to me. I congratulate her, you, and myself, heartily, upon your being able to add that most welcome postscript concerning the state of your health. May it long continue thus excellent, is the sincere trust of

MARY COWDEN CLARKE.

JAN. 18, 1854,
27 PORCHESTER TERRACE, BAYSWATER.

MY DEAR ENTHUSIAST:

CHARLES'S visit to Aske Hall, which is near to Richmond in Yorkshire, was in every respect most delightful. His noble host and hostess treated him with distinguished courtesy and kindness, while their titled guests followed their example. It was a pleasant instance of the

[213]

consideration with which a man of letters is received among people of rank — and at the same time of intelligence and good taste. I believe the family name of the Earl of Zetland was originally Dundas. Charles says Lady Zetland is extremely handsome, and nothing could exceed the grace of her behaviour towards him throughout. Two of the evenings the lectures were delivered to the company staying at the Hall; but on one of the three the Earl had invited the members of the Mechanics' Institution near him, and a large number of the neighbouring gentry and tenantry, so as to afford the treat of hearing the lecture to as many as possible. Liberal and kindly, was it not? Altogether Charles's account of his sojourn there was most interesting. At the end of this month he leaves home again, on his Scottish tour, — which is to comprise courses at Alexandria, Dumbarton, Falkirk, Stirling, and Kirkcudbright, — and then begins his North of England tour, which is to include courses at Carlisle, Bradford, Wakefield, Leeds, Sheffield, and Barnsley. You may imagine I don't like parting with him for so long a period; but as fame and profit are both advanced by these absences, I have no right to complain of them.

How you rejoice me, my dear sir, by the assur-

ance that your health continues so excellent!
Long may it be preserved. I shall hope to send
you by post or parcel soon three enchanting articles of our admired friend Leigh Hunt's writing,
which have appeared in the " Musical Times "
lately. They are penned with all his old — or
rather young — vigour and warmth of enthusiasm. He is a glorious spirit! With loving
regards to your dear wife, believe me to be

Your affectionate
MARY COWDEN CLARKE.

FEB. 2ND, 1854,
27 PORCHESTER TERRACE, BAYSWATER.

MY DEAR ENTHUSIAST:

I AM going to claim your fulfilment of a kind
promise you made me, that if I would let
you know the subject of my next book, you
would do your best for me about an American
publisher, — adding, " Mr. Putnam is beyond
all doubt the most liberal; but I would try several, both here and at Philadelphia and Boston."
Now, I venture to ask the favour of you to
take this trouble on behalf of your daughter-in-
love, leaving it entirely to you to pursue the
means which appear to you most judicious; as
well as the arrangement of what sum I am to

receive for the transmission of proofs by advance steamer, — gratefully remembering how kindly you arranged matters for me before, in the case of the "Girlhood." The title of my new book is "The Iron Cousin; or Mutual Influence." It is to form one of Routledge's two-volume series, the size of which you doubtless know.

Charles is awa to bonnie Scotland. I have heard from him to say he had safely arrived at Glasgow, on his way to Alexandria, Dumbartonshire. Our news from Nice and Milan are excellent, thank God! To-day is almost a Nice day — quite a *nice* one — oh! — blue sky, shining sun, air with the blandness of spring. My mother's accounts of the weather there are enchanting. Winter is scarcely winter in Nice; it is so mitigated in severity, so shortened in duration. She writes me that my sister Emma finds the sun too powerful for walking, so she sits out upon the seashore and waits till the carriage comes to take her up, to enjoy my mother's drive with her. There is a valley a mile or two off from my mother's campagna which I wish you could see; enclosed within such fine bold crags, — Shelley's Goethe's "giant mounted crags," — and itself so luxuriant with foliage and green-embowered beauty. There is a grotto there, with silver-dropping, natural fountain, behung with a profusion of mosses and ferns, that is worth a pilgrimage to behold. This valley is one of Niobe's favourite drives. Clara once joined us in some open-air music that my father has set for us, when we spent a day in that lovely spot. It was a time to remember. So true are Keats's words: "A thing of beauty is a joy forever."

I must not take another sheet of paper, or I should go gossiping on "from morn to dewy eve;" so will conclude. I am

Your affectionate

MARY COWDEN CLARKE.

Kindest remembrances to Mrs. Balmanno. Ask her to tell me how the name of my new book strikes her.

MY DEAR SIR:

THE bearer of this note is Mr. Routledge, well known to my brother Alfred, to me as the publisher of my new book, and to the world as the spirited purchaser of Sir Bulwer Lytton's works. Any information with which you can supply him in furtherance of his views in visiting America will be an additional favour to those already conferred upon, my dear sir,

Yours, faithfully and obliged,

MARY COWDEN CLARKE.

ROBERT BALMANNO, ESQ.

LETTERS TO AN ENTHUSIAST

*The two letters which follow were published, when received by
Mr. Balmanno, in an American newspaper.*

MAY 30, 1854,
27 PORCHESTER TERRACE, BAYSWATER.

MY DEAR ENTHUSIAST :

I REJOICE to learn that you are quite recovered from your spring attack of indisposition. Long may you preserve health and strength.
No, my dear sir, I have *not* read about the
grand electric light manufactory at Wandsworth.
I have told Alf to bear in mind your wish respecting any particular account of it that may
appear ; also relative to the best and fullest description of that " World's Wonder, the Sydenham Exhibition," as you truly call it. I am in
hopes that I shall be able to send you my own
personal account of the latter's opening day, as
Alf has obtained the proud privilege for us Trihominate of having our names put down on the
list of choral performers on that occasion. Fortunately, Charles's and my own figured on a certain card once printed, when Beethoven's Grand
Mass in D — reckoned the most difficult music
ever composed — was first performed in England,
at Mr. A——'s in Queen Square, in the year
1832 ; so we have an honourable voucher for
our being able to take part in a vocal perform-

[218]

ance. Clara and her husband were going to ask
for the same privilege — looking upon it as one,
for the sake of being present; but a little bird
whispered, that instead of asking, she would be
asked; and moreover, to sing a *solo* verse in the
National Anthem — a most distinguished honour,
especially under the peculiar circumstances. For
it was averred that no human voice was capable
of being heard in that enormous space; but if
any, it was " the Novello's." Accordingly, Costa
asked her to come down quietly to Sydenham
last Sunday morning and meet him, to ascertain
the exact truth of the matter, and make a trial
of her voice in the Crystal Palace. She and
her husband, Charles and I, drove down in her
carriage, through the charming Dulwich lanes,
and Alf, [having arranged] for a substitute in
his choir, joined us by railway. Costa was punctual; and we had not been five minutes in the
building before he and Gigliucci went over to the
other end of the great transept, far beyond where
the Queen's dais is to be, while we stood with
Clara, on the spot where the orchestra will
be stationed. The experiment answered tri-
umphantly; her voice rang out pure and large
and trumpet-like. Costa shouted gleefully his
confirmation in Italian, while he and Gigliucci
came hurrying back, the expression on their

faces fully showing the complete success of the
trial. It has always been affirmed that no single
voice could make itself effectively heard in that
vast edifice; and now Clara's is pronounced the
one that can! We all exclaimed " Ah, if Niobe
were but here, how her heart would swell with
motherly pride and joy!" Afterwards Clara
made a further trial, for our own private satisfaction; and what do you think it was? She
went to the extreme one end of the edifice, and
Charles, Alf, and I went to the extreme other
end. The first building measured 1,851 feet
in length, and this one many feet longer. It
was so far that at last we could only see her
a speck in the distance. When she arrived,
she telegraphed to us, by waving her parasol, —
a white one, which Niobe had embroidered for
her with a wreath of green oak-leaves when
she was last in Nice, — and I answered by waving mine in reply. Then she sang the verse;
and the effect was one of the most curious I
ever heard in my life, and almost supernaturally
beautiful. It was like an angel — clear, sweet,
exquisitely distinct, but remote. " God save
our gracious Queen!" It came thrilling and
vibrant, but singularly distinct; it produced an
impression that I shall never forget, if I live a
hundred years. How I would long that our

beloved mother could have been there to have heard her child utter such wondrous proof of the glorious gift that God has bestowed upon her. We always knew that Clara's voice was extraordinarily powerful in combination with its delicious sweetness; but we never could have believed the extent of its power, had we not actually made this curious experiment. Charles and Alf both actually smiled when she proposed it; they could hardly believe it possible that a human organ could be heard, when we measured the extent with our eyes. We had rather a curious additional proof again later. For, after we five had been rambling about, enjoying the admirable assemblage of grand beauties brought together there under one roof, — the Alhambra court, the Greek court, the Italian court, the Pompeian court, etc., — several distinguished gentle-men belonging to the Crystal Palace, such as Sir Joseph Paxton, Sir Charles Fox, and others, arrived; and after Clara had been introduced to those among them she did not already know, and had stood talking to them all some little time, she was asked whether she could be prevailed upon to repeat the trial-verse, that they might hear and enjoy it also. She had no sooner acceded and sung it through once more than several visitors, who had by this time come, and were dispersed about the building, came flocking up the aisles, thus affording strong proof how the tones penetrated into all parts of the place. You may imagine how happily we all drove home together, chatting her triumph over.

I have scribbled so much upon this theme that I have hardly left myself room to tell you that I enclose a specimen (they are only in proof, but they will serve to give you an idea of the plan, and I know you are interested in the Sydenham "Wonder of the World") of the letters Alf intends to have upon his show-case for the stationery court there. It will afford a good sample of his types, and form something new and original in its effect. The word " Novello's " will be in letter type, you see; and the word "Music" is to be in music type. They are to be in scarlet, so as to produce a vivid relief upon the plate glass, backed by specimen pages of white music-paper. He is very much pleased with his situation; it is in the stationery court, near the centre entrance; so that all those passing down the centre aisle will see the case.

You ask why I always write by the Cunard steamers. I merely send my letters to the post-office, and *they* decide what steamer my letter goes by. I generally write by the Friday's post.

But to-day, as I do not wish to delay, I write by the Tuesday's.

Believe me always to be

Your grateful

M. C. C.

JUNE 15, 1854,

27 PORCHESTER TERRACE, BAYSWATER.

MY DEAR ENTHUSIAST:

YOU will doubtless have seen an account of Saturday's ceremonial from the English newspapers, which I understand are all full of it; but as I know your paternal partiality is given to attach an affectionate importance to your daughter-in-love's description, she will be your "own correspondent" on the occasion, since she had the privilege of being present. I think I told you that we Trihominate were invited to take part in the musical performance; and most admirably were all the orchestral arrangements planned. I enclose you the private particulars, as they may interest you to look at. We had not the slightest difficulty, either in getting down by the train, or reaching our places when arrived. The Crystal Palace itself was a perfect fairy scene. The rich assemblage of colour, the ladies' gala dresses, the myriads of flowers, the plants, the statuary, the universal ground of glowing

crimson — for all the avenues through which the
Royal procession was to pass were laid down
with red cloth — formed a brilliant combination
rarely beheld in our climate, especially as over all
the sun shone with the brightness of a Southern
atmosphere. Then the Queen arrived, shedding
even more lustre upon the scene by her kind and
graciously beaming countenance than by her
slender court environments. As she ascended
the dais, the introductory symphony to the National Anthem — newly and most effectively
arranged by Costa for the occasion — pealed
forth; and then, clear, distinct, pure, and powerful, came Clara's beautiful voice, uttering the
people's universal aspiration — "God save the
Queen!" One curious and interesting circumstance I noticed, and that was that, just as
Clara rang out that fine thrilling high note, at
the close of the first strain, the stroke of the
first cannon boomed forth at the same instant.
The effect was electrical. Not only was my
own sisterly heart moved with delight and excitement, but all that vast audience testified their
admiration at the noble way in which the supremacy of Clara's tones asserted itself on this
great occasion. Numerous friends afterwards
overwhelmed her with congratulations, and even
from strangers we had curious proof of the effect

she produced. One among several other in-
stances: As Gigliucci, Clara, Charles, and I were
going home together in the train a party of
ladies and gentlemen got into the same carriage.
There was such a scramble returning that we got
into a second-class, notwithstanding our first-class
tickets, and so it seems had these other people;
and they began talking over the day's delight.
At length they became eloquent in their praises
of Madame Novello's singing of " God save the
Queen," one of the gentlemen declaring that for
his part, he thought that was the greatest treat
of the whole. Presently one of the ladies turned
to Charles, and asked him if he did n't agree
with them in thinking Madame Novello's singing the finest thing of the entertainment, when
he very quietly assented, and then added, " That 's
she in the corner opposite us." The lady looked
at first a little startled, as one does when one has
been giving an opinion very freely of a person
in their presence, and then she said to Charles
(Clara and I were talking to each other, so did
not hear the whispered colloquy between Charles
and the strange lady), " Do you think Madame
Novello would feel offended if I were to tell her
how much we had been delighted?" "What
person ever was displeased by a kind compliment?" returned Charles. Whereupon the lady

bent forward, and in the prettiest manner begged
to thank Clara for the great pleasure she had
given them all. Then the gentlemen and the
other lady of the party discovered whom she was
speaking to, and they joined in, with some
equally courteous acknowledgment. It was very
gratifying, as you may imagine; and this was
only one of the many pleasant things of the
kind that occurred to us during the day. The
whispers that reached us, the glances thrown at
her as she passed, etc., gave plentiful token of
the universal admiration her singing so finely in
that vast space had produced. On Monday, as
Alf chanced to be in an omnibus, he heard a
country gentleman near him, evidently come up
to town for a holiday, and at last he said: "But
that young woman that sang the bit by herself,
in 'God save the Queen,' she was the best of
all. You could hear her all over the place, and
yet so sweet." That same night he happened to
meet Mr. Cobden, relative to the "Taxes on
Knowledge" business, and Mr. C. said: "There
are only two things talked of in the House this
evening — your sister's singing on Saturday and
our advertisement." You will think I am horribly egotistical, telling you so much about the
one subject that interests me; but I can think
of hardly anything else, ever since, and I know I

may let my thoughts take their course, and my tongue — or rather *pen* — run when I am gossiping with my indulgent father-in-love.

The Queen looked remarkably well, and behaved with her usual kind courtesy; she looked round more than once, as Clara sang, and afterwards, as she passed the orchestra, gave two distinct bows towards it. She always takes a gracious pleasure in marking her delighted acceptance of the efforts made to gratify her, and especially so where music is concerned. Our Queen Victoria's conduct on these occasions always makes me think of those generous kingly words that our idol Shakespeare has put into the Royal Theseus's mouth in the first scene of the fifth act of " Midsummer Night's Dream," beginning : " The kinder we," etc.[1] The body of voices and the fine choral and instrumental effects of Handel's glorious " Hallelujah " produced a magnificent effect, and the Royal hearers paid pointed attention to its performance, while it was going on. It was a genuine delight to me, the taking part in it, and joining my unit of a voice to the hundreds that swelled the mighty sound. It was

---

[1] " The kinder we, to give them thanks for nothing.
Our sport shall be to take what they mistake:
And what poor duty cannot do, noble respect
Takes it in might, not merit ! "

a day never to be forgotten, an era in one's life.

We have not yet been able to meet with any account of the grand electric light manufactory at Wandsworth which you mention in your last; but should we do so, we will not fail to remember your wish to have it. I have told Alf to bear it in mind. Our accounts from Nice continue good of our beloved Niobe's health. How she would have enjoyed being present on Saturday!

I omitted in my last, I believe, to reply to your query as to the paragraph relative to the " Merry Wives " festival in honour of Shakespeare's birthday. Yes, dear sir, I saw the paragraph, but the festival, I fancy, only took place in a certain Enthusiast's brain, where

> " Imagination bodies forth
> The forms of things unknown " [1]

to prosaic reality. You also, with your usual kind thought, sent me a paper containing an account of the sale of the "Girlhood" by Mr. Putnam. I am ashamed to own that I omitted to put this paper into the box with my other American documents, in consequence of which it has been mislaid and I forgot the name of the

---

[1] " Midsummer Night's Dream," Act V, Scene I.

"Girlhood" purchaser. Will you kindly tell me
again what that name is in your next letter? I
fear I shall run some risk of sending this by
the same line of steamers as those you forbade
me to forward by; but I am obliged to post my
letters without knowing particulars, so forgive
me! I generally find the Friday's post more con-
venient to me than the Tuesday's, as Monday is
with me a more busy day, generally, than Thursday. One can hardly account for these things,
but so it is; methodical people find themselves
oddly trammelled by their peculiarities of order
sometimes, and one of my impudent girl-friends
once told me I was "an old maid spoiled." She
thinks me methodical to a fault, and so perhaps
I am, but nevertheless,

Your affectionate

M. C. C.

------

*Letter written by Charles Cowden Clarke to Mr. Balmanno
after the death of his wife's mother.*

SEPT. 4TH, 1854,
LONDON, 69 DEAN STREET, SOHO.

MY DEAR MR. BALMANNO:

YOUR two mournful newspapers have this day
come to hand; and I daresay in the course
of a few days — perhaps this week — my Molly will
acknowledge your kind and graceful record of the mel-
ancholy bereavement we have all experienced. Alfred

[229]

is with the Gigliuccis, who are at Worcester, preparing
for the Festival, which commences to-morrow. You
are perfectly correct in your account of the dreadful
suddenness of the news, for we were to have started
for Nice on the very day — the 31st July — on which
we received Gigliucci's letter. But, my dear sir, it was
sudden only to Mary and Alf. The Gigliuccis took
the kind precaution — knowing the day we were to
start — to send a telegraphic message from Genoa,
desiring us not to leave England till we had their
letter of the 26th, which was to reach us on the 31st.
Such is the sanguine and non-evil-anticipating character of Alf's and his sister's natures, that they apprehended no more from this telegraphic despatch than
that it was some commissions from the Gigliuccis.
I apprehended the worst; and miserable enough I
was from the Thursday till the following Monday,
the 31st; and when I found the promised letter did
not come to Bayswater, my apprehensions became
confirmed. I went alone to Dean Street, and there
it was. Well, I returned immediately, of course, to
Bayswater, and, to my bitter feeling, I found them
both in the highest spirits, laughing at the prospect of
some trick they were to play their mother; and upon
my entering, Molly said, "Here he comes to tell us
to pack up." You may imagine the result, for I could
not dissemble. I never in my life saw anything more
affecting, and more simple and childlike, than their
grief; for never did I witness any filial love more reverential, more affectionate, and more genuine than that
of Vincent and Mary Sabilla Novello's children; and

this I firmly believe to be one cause of the uniform prosperity of the whole family. The youngest of the family is Mary Sabilla, and she it was that was with her mother. Clara also, most fortunately, was there too. Emma was and is still in Paris, with a daughter of Roll's, the eminent Chancery barrister. There is no bigger and sounder head in the whole brood than Sabilla's, and no sounder heart either; she is a fine creature. She is a sound musician, an extraordinary artist, and as familiar with the French, Italian, Spanish, and German languages as her native English.

And now, my dear sir, I have, in turn, to condole with you upon the loss of your old and esteemed friend, Crofton Croker. Poor fellow! the painful operation he dreaded I suppose carried him off. In the case of our beloved one, — although it was cholera, it was so rapid, and she being so very feeble a subject, there was little or nothing for the disease to lay hold of, she was taken after breakfast of the 25th July, and was gone before the 26th. Strange to say, there were no discolorations; and after death, Clara says that the most exquisite smile with — for some time — a light flush was on her countenance. I am happy to say that the family are all returning to good health.

Present my kind compliments to Mrs. Balmanno; and accept yourself, my dear sir, every kind feeling from

Yours, very faithful and obliged,
C. COWDEN CLARKE.

SEPT. 14, 1854,
27 PORCHESTER TERRACE, BAYSWATER.

MY DEAR ENTHUSIAST:

I HAVE not had courage before to write to you; but your short note of Aug. 29th just received makes me feel I ought to do so. The agitation and incoherence of the note, dear sir, formed a better self-evident token of affectionate sympathy than any more studied assurance could have done. Thank you from my heart for it; yours will tell you why I cannot say more on the subject.

I received the copy of the " New York Daily Times " for Aug. 21st, which you kindly sent me, but not the paper you mention in your last note. For all, my truest thanks. I received, in due course, your letters of the 30th July and of the 5th Aug., one of which contained a cutout advertisement of " Iron Cousin." For all these tokens of your kind thought of me and my interests accept my grateful acknowledgments.

My Charles tells me he wrote to you lately, that your immediate anxiety respecting us might be relieved; but I think you will be interested to know how we are all going on. Dear noble Clara made the necessary exertion to fulfil her engagements at the provincial festivals; for the sake of

those she loves, and that she might not disappoint the public, she bravely resolved to go through with it all. She and her husband arrived in England, bringing our dear Sabilla with them; she is my youngest sister, not Emma. The latter was in Paris at the time of our loss — for whom we had great fears, her health not being strong. Sabilla was to have gone with Clara to the festivals, as we hoped that the call upon her energies might be of service; but they were all — Sabilla and the Gigliuccis — seized with so severe an attack of this prevailing malady, though, thank God, not in its most fatal form, that after visiting with them two nights at their hotel, and nursing them all three, I persuaded Sybil to give up accompanying the Gigliuccis out of town, and come here instead, while Alf accompanied Clara to Worcester and Norwich, as a support to her and her husband, in case of a relapse. Thank God their health has been quite restored, and Clara's voice was never in finer and stronger order; so that her noble courage has had its best reward. Dear Sybil also benefited by the quiet sojourn here with Charles and me. The repose — even to dulness — has been best medicine to her, while the needful thought and attention I have been called upon for have had their advantage for me. In addition to my nursing duties I have had the care of my poor dear father fall to my share. He is with us, and the seeing that he has every wish prevented has been a salutary occupation. It is not only a comfort in itself, but it is something to do for *her* sake. Our chief solicitude just now is for dear Sabilla. The shock falls perhaps most severely upon her. She was our beloved mother's constant companion for the last five years, and was her darling Benjamin. We would fain keep dear Sybil with us; it would be so deep a comfort to us all, for she is as kind-hearted as she is gentle-hearted, while in return she feels many points in strong sympathy with us. But her health will not bear a winter in England, and she thinks of returning to Nice — at any rate this season. Alf will see her back after the Gigliuccis return from the provinces.

Dear Clara has sent me up from Worcester a most interesting gift: it is no other than a Shakespeare jug. I have been so much pleased with it that I have written down to Worcester to order one for you, my dear sir; I hope you will receive it in due course, and that you will accept it as a loving remembrance from your affectionate daughter-in-love. Alf, dear fellow, writes me a daily line, letting me know how Clara gets through her arduous task. They are at Norwich this week, were at Worcester and Birmingham last week, and will go on to Liverpool, ready for the opening of St. George's Hall next week.

We felt acutely for you, my dear sir, in anticipation of the blow we found was in store for you, when we learned the death of excellent Mr. Crofton Croker; we knew how you loved and esteemed him, and fully sympathized with the pain we knew you would feel in his loss. Take heart against your grief, however, my dear father-in-love, for the sake of those who love you, for the sake of your dear wife and sons, for the sake of your attached friends, among whom none has reason to be more gratefully loving than

MARY COWDEN CLARKE.

ROBERT BALMANNO, ESQ.

DEC. 23, 1854,

27 PORCHESTER TERRACE, BAYSWATER.

MY DEAR ENTHUSIAST:

YOUR kind letter of the 13th reached me through the obliging medium of Mr. Dillon Croker. Many thanks for it, and for the one bearing date of November 25th. These two letters and the papers you are so good as to send us make me feel very like a delinquent in not hav-

ing written to you lately. . . . I have more than
once had it said to me, you will readily guess by
whom, — only one who is a lover and a husband
at the same time, — " I wonder what you could
do, that I'd not forgive; " and when my Enthusiast follows up this sort of spoiling with similar
indulgence, as he does, I naturally feel secure
of pardon even when I am remiss in letter
punctuality.

It rejoices me to know — as I find by your last
letters, describing the inscription and the case
— that you are so well pleased with the little
jug. But you made your daughter-in-love smile
when she read your account of what you had
had engraved upon the lid, and then fancied you
might hug yourself upon its passing for the
donor's inscription. Why, my dear Enthusiast,
the very form of it betrays you. " Mary Cowden
Clarke to Robert Balmanno." Whereas, if she
had had it engraved, it would naturally have run
thus: " Robert Balmanno from Mary Cowden
Clarke." Now that's what I call a piece of
woman's subtlety for you! Seriously, however,
I am only too proud and pleased to think that
you value the trifle sufficiently to mark your liking for it in the affectionate way you have done.
Your account of the American ladies' idea of its
having been used for molasses amused us greatly.

I fancy dear Willie quaffing good Warwickshire ale from its lips, when he was too thirsty to wait for a glass; remember it had no cover in his time. Perhaps a recollection of his draughts from this very jug haunted his thoughts when he wrote that passionate adjuration of Master Kit Sly's:[1] "For God's sake, a pot of small ale!" or that almost more fervent and most natural ejaculation of Falstaff's boy in the thick of the battle: "I would give all my fame for a pot of ale and safety!"[2] Imagine Shakespeare, the immortal poet, so merged in the mortal man as to lovingly "remember the poor creature, small beer," in his thirsty transport, and be willing to give up all *his* fame for a pot of ale — cool, sparkling, delicious Warwickshire ale!

You ask me if I knew Charles Lamb. I thank God, I did. This very enthusiasm about the malt beverage reminds me of pleasant things in my privileged intercourse with him. I was an honoured partaker in one of those country walks of his, when he would stop at some little roadside inn, and have some cool porter. He preferred porter and ale, and I remember his especially expressing his approval of my taste when I ventured to second his commendation of

---

[1] " Taming of the Shrew," Induction, Scene II.
[2] " Henry V," Act III, Scene II.

Barclay and Perkins's porter as superior to any other brewer's. I think he liked that a girl should have an opinion in porter, and not be afraid of avowing it. I recollect our once stopping at some wayside hostelry near Waltham Cross, and his drinking " the memory of Harold " as our toast on that occasion. On another, my father chose to defray the " score for sheer ale "[1] (porter), and Charles Lamb said, " Do, Novello; I shall like the draught all the better for it."

In one of these green lane walks, admirable Miss Kelly happened to be at Enfield with us that day; and I remember his being pleased that both she and I sat in the little porch and pledged him, while he had the beer brought there. He always liked to see women superior to fine lady-ism and affectation, though no one had a truer appreciation of real feminine refinement. I recollect his trying me with one of his whimsical ways in that kind of test once. Charles and I were down at Enfield for a few days, and went one evening with himself and his beloved sister Mary to drink tea with some people who had invited them both. Charles Lamb and I chanced to outwalk my Charles and Miss Lamb, and we arrived first at the house, a ladies' school. The lady of the house received us politely, and ex-

---

[1] " Taming of the Shrew," Induction, Scene II.

pressed herself pleased to see — bowing to me
— any friend of Mr. Lamb's with him. He
answered her inquiry after his sister, by saying
that she had a horrible toothache, and had
stayed at home; and Mr. C. C. had remained
to keep her company. And then he added,
"His wife and I, as we came along, were hoping
that you might have sprats for supper to-night,
Mrs. ——." You might imagine the effect that
this produced, in a somewhat prim company —
assemblage; but I could see that he was pleased
at my not being in the slightest discomposed at
this singular introduction to a strange lady, in a
strange house. I have sometimes thought that
I owe it to the gratitude I feel for having known
two such glorious beings, to jot down all my
reminiscences of beloved Charles Lamb and his
excellent sister Mary. She was worthy to be his
sister; and that is saying everything. You ask
me if there is any monumental stone over his
grave. Yes; it is in the little village church-
yard at Edmonton; and the lines on the tomb-
stone are by Wordsworth. But Charles does
not think them worthy of Lamb's memory.[1]

---

[1] " Farewell, dear friend ; that smile, that harmless mirth,
   No more shall gladden our domestic hearth ;
   That rising tear, with pain forbid to flow,
   Better than words, no more assuage our woe;

You ask me whether I know who is the present editor of the " Examiner." I have been told that it is John Forster, the author of that charming " Life of Goldsmith," and the enactor of Master Ford in the memorable amateur performance of " Merry Wives " in 1848. I believe he has long written the literary critiques in the " Examiner," and they are excellent. I felt honoured by the notice he gave the " Iron Cousin," for I value his opinion very highly. I will confess to my father-in-love that this notice of Mr. Forster's in the " Examiner," and still more a pencilled note written by dear Leigh Hunt on the blank leaf of our own copy which Charles lent him to read, gave me more pleasure than anything that has occurred to me this year, of that kind. Excuse this egoism.

I hope you are enjoying as fine a season in New York as we are having here. The weather is, most days, as bright and clear, really sunny, as though it were not midwinter. But I suppose

That hand outstretched from small but well-earned store
Yields succour to the destitute no more.
Yet art thou not all lost; through many an age,
With sterling sense and humour, shall thy page
Win many an English bosom, pleased to see
That old and happier vein revived in thee.
This for our earth; and if with friends we share
Our joys in heaven, we hope to meet thee there."

at the turn of the year we shall have some fierce cold.

That miserable war [1] makes everything very dull and very dear. It is lamentable to see the prevalence of mourning wear; it makes my heart ache. Those who have been the means of prompting so fearful an affliction upon their human brethren, for interested party purposes and selfish individual gain, have a terrible crime to answer for.

With every kindest and sincerest wish of Xmas enjoyment and New Year blessing, to Mrs. Balmanno and yourself, from the Trihominate, believe me to be

Your affectionate
MARY COWDEN CLARKE.

ROBERT BALMANNO, ESQ.

MAR. 8, 1855,
27 PORCHESTER TERRACE, BAYSWATER.

MY DEAR ENTHUSIAST:

YOUR kind letter of the 6th February was only grievous in one thing, its bringing me an account of your having been ill. But thank God, you were already better, and I trust by this time you are your hearty self again. Many thanks for my father-in-love's "true and fervent

---

[1] The Crimean War.

prayer." A blessing like that, breathed by a father's heart, must be precious.

I agree with you respecting the fascination of Miss Kelly's eyes; her brow was one of the most expressive I ever saw, and her speaking voice was absolute perfection. Did I ever send you a copy of a little sketch of her acting that I once wrote for a friend, to insert in a county paper where she was about to give a dramatic reading? It is most probable I did, as it might interest you, who knew and admired her.

No, my dear sir, I have not received the Philadelphian application which you anticipate, with respect to my " career." But, curiously enough, about a week or so after I received your letter, I had a similar request from an English lady, who has been applied to by an English publisher to get up something of the kind you allude to. As this kind of request involves a compliment, one can do no other than respond to them courteously; I therefore sent her what simple particulars there were to supply.

Clara and her husband are returning to England, leaving dear Sabilla and their children all well, I am thankful to say. Dear Emma is also in London, still with the youngest Miss Roll for the present. My Charles has just departed on a long lecture tour in the North of England and bonnie Scotland, which will detain him absent for a long space of time. I do not expect him home until Easter. I ought to rejoice, and so I do, professionally; but domestically and conjugally, I rather regret. For life seems growing too short to allow such great slices out of one's time for being together on earth. However, one learns patience and submission as one grows older; for every day's experience brings a lesson that we are not to have all we wish.

Pray present our united kindest compliments and best regards to Mrs. Balmanno, together with those jointly offered to yourself, and believe me to be　　　Your affectionate

MARY COWDEN CLARKE.

APRIL 5, 1855,
27 PORCHESTER TERRACE, BAYSWATER.

MY DEAR ENTHUSIAST:

I SHOULD indeed have very much wondered (but I think I must be out of my wits before I'd think you "unkind") had I received a letter from Brooklyn without a word from you at the same time. Your settling it so decidedly that the Czar is not only dead but d——d amuses me extremely. It reminds me of Congreve's petulance, who, when they damned his play of "The Way of the World," assured the audi-

[243]

ence, in a neat and appropriate speech, that that comedy would live when they were all dead and d——d.

You will find, by my letter to your dear wife, that her rival is out of the field. Alfred, yesterday only, received intelligence that the last number of the paper was issued, and that it had died from want of capital. There was no question, however, of d——g as well as dying; so the name is not blasted if you think fit to revive it. But perhaps the best way would be to adopt some other that should embody the general idea of Mrs. Balmanno's book; and none seems better than the one she herself proposed. You will see the modification I have suggested. I trust that whatever you and she may ultimately decide upon, it may prove the very best. . . .

M. C. C.

SEPT. 2ND, 1855,
27 PORCHESTER TERRACE, BAYSWATER.

MY DEAR ENTHUSIAST:

"MY conscience, hanging about the neck of my heart,"[1] is beginning to upbraid me for not having written to you since the 15th of July. I hope you got that letter safely; for though there was nothing particular in it, yet

---

[1] "Merchant of Venice," Act II, Scene II.

had you not received it, you must have accused
me of neglect in correspondence. The fact is, I
have no news to send ; and I seem to have lost all
spirit for fabricating letters out of nothing. Life
— my life, at least — has become a dull daily
duty-doing, now that it has lost one of its dearest
charms. We are all here, well in health, thank
God. Sabilla is with us, and very much better
and stronger this year, I am happy to say. She
enjoys herself as much as she ever does in England, disliking the climate so extremely. She
and the Gigliuccis labour hard to convert us to
their preference for the Italian heat. Alfred is
fast coming round to their views; for he finds
the severity of the winters here tries him greatly.
They persuade me, also, that my Charles feels
the cold of the English climate keenly, knowing
that the health of those I love is always the first
consideration with me. I suppose it will end in
my giving up my predilection for old England,
as far as consenting to go with them all to live
in Italy, whenever they decide to do so. And
really, after all, so that they are well and happy
and I am with them, I have grown to care little
for all else. I trust wholly to your own kind
heart to comprehend the thanks I feel towards
you, and to believe that I am, in all truth, your
affectionate   MARY COWDEN CLARKE.

JAN. 21, 1856,
27 PORCHESTER TERRACE, BAYSWATER.

MY DEAR ENTHUSIAST:

I CANNOT sufficiently thank you for sending me that Boston paper containing the collection of articles upon my tragic idol, Rachel. Do you know who wrote them? They recall to me so many of her great scenes. I have seen her in all the characters there enumerated, with the exception of those in the "Moineau de Lesbie" and in Angelo. Hermione was the second in which I have seen her, Roxane being the first, in Racine's "Bajazet," which play she does not seem to have acted while in America. She reminded me most of Edmund Kean, in this last character; but she does not seem to have performed it lately. The only time I ever saw her off the stage was once, in the waiting-room at the Annerly Station. I was with Clara; we had been to a private view of the Crystal Palace before it was opened. I was standing on the platform with Gigliucci and Alfred, when Charles and Clara came to us, and the latter said in her low voice to me, "Victoria, do you know who is in that room?" — pointing quietly to the waiting-room near — "As I passed through I saw Rachel and her brother, with a party, sitting there; and I knew you would

[246]

never forgive me if I did not tell you of it." I hurried softly back, and there I saw the glorious, serious face. She raised her fine dark eyes, and they met mine. I could hardly resist the desire I had to go up to her and say, "J'ai a vous remercier de m'avoir fait pleurer maintes fois;" but my besetting foible of shyness was too strong, and I could not muster courage to address her.

Alfred has gone to Nice for a few weeks, to have a Southern holiday with Sabilla, and to prepare for building some additional rooms, which the house will require when we all repair thither. I fancy this will take place next autumn. I can only trust that this removal will conduce to our mutual family happiness; at any rate, the Gigliuccis, Sabilla, and Alf are pleased at the prospect of living there; and Charles and I will learn to like it for their sake. My kind Enthusiast and father-in-love will be equally able to write to me there as here; and his correspondence will, I trust, continue to delight his grateful

MARY COWDEN CLARKE.

JUNE 8, 1856,
27 PORCHESTER TERRACE, BAYSWATER.

MY DEAR ENTHUSIAST:

I HAVE to thank you for the pleasure of forming the acquaintance of several delightful people. Mr. Knightly favoured me with a visit, and I had some charming conversation with him. He is quite the scholar and gentleman, the refined and quiet student. He read me a very amusing extract from one of Mrs. Balmanno's letters, which he had lately received, where she tells him a story of a wayfarer coolly asking her for food, and stating that he liked his eggs "boiled lightly"!

AUG. 8, 1856,
UGBROOKE PARK, DEVONSHIRE.

I WRITE to you from here because I think you will be pleased to receive a letter from so charming a place. My health has been not good, and change of air and scene was advised. My Aunt Catherine kindly invited the Trihominate to pay a visit of a week or so, and we are now enjoying the intense delight of this noble mansion and demain. Lord Clifford is generously pleased to mark the light in which he regards my aunt, by allowing her to welcome her family

[248]

here while he is absent from England, he himself
residing constantly in Rome for many years past.
My aunt had the charge of his two youngest
sons, when death deprived them of their mother;
and his lordship has always been prompt to acknowledge my aunt's tender and judicious care
of them. Thus, we visit Ugbrooke under peculiarly pleasant circumstances. But the place
itself, my dear sir, is a paradise to people of our
tastes and feelings. The fine old house, with
its lofty rooms, its long corridors, its spacious
hall and staircase, its quiet chapel with the silver
lamp ever burning before the shrine; the stately
library adjoining, where I am at present writing,
and where the windows command a glorious
view; the magnificent park, with its swelling
uplands and grassy lawns, crowned with trees
and grouped with herds of deer; the broad sheet
of water, on which a swan

> " with arched neck
> Between her white wings mantling proudly, rows
> Her state with oary feet," —

all combine to form one of those perfect spots
which perhaps only people like ourselves, with
arduous avocations yet love of leisure, with artistic tastes yet moderate means, fully and intensely
appreciate. There are some fine paintings in
the drawing-room suite, the most renowned of

which is a "Woman taken in adultery," by Titian. But my favourite picture is a "Repose," by Gentileschi. The attitude of the mother is the consummation of grace and natural ease; while the expression of the countenances, both mother's and child's, is matchless for truth and vividness. My men-folk both are enjoying themselves thoroughly. Charles pores over the curious old volumes here in the library, and gives a touch to the ivory balls in the billiard-room near, as he passes through, and lounges beside the windows enjoying the peerless view; while Alf looks over the fishing rods and tackle with Emma, or strays down by the lake, in green shady nooks with her, watching his line while she sketches; and between whiles we chat with Aunt Catherine, and of an evening read to her, or sing some of our favourite four-part music, without accompaniment, to her. In short, we revel in all its luxury of tranquil pleasure, to our heart's content; and as for me, my health is stronger and my spirits better than they have been for many a long month.

I received your letter dated 10th June — Clara's birthday — duly, and trust the next I receive from you may contain more satisfactory tidings of the progress made by Mrs. Balmanno's book, in the matter of publication. That is generally the least agreeable part of an author's work. But there had need, in justice, be some counterbalance to the pleasure there is in writing a work. That is the author's share of enjoyment; that is the author's true delight. God bless you, and preserve you in health and happiness, my dear kind friend, is the sincere prayer of

MARY COWDEN CLARKE.

AUG. 15, 1856,
27 PORCHESTER TERRACE, BAYSWATER.

MY DEAR ENTHUSIAST:

YOUR delightful letter of the 22nd July was forwarded to me at Ugbrooke Park. On my return home here, I found the dainty little packet, containing the elegant little gift, that exquisite daguerreotype of Shakespeare in its beautiful case. Charles and I both agree that we have not seen a more tasteful thing altogether for many a long day. Accept our united thanks for it, my dear sir; it will, with other of your kind and generous presents, accompany us to Nice, and help to adorn our new home there.

You ask where I acquired my methodical habits. I think very likely they were inherited from my father, who in his days of youth and energy was one of the most industrious and punctual of men. I have known him correct proofs of his various musical works late at night, after a party, or an evening at the theatre. He played the organ at the Portuguese chapel for a period of six-and-twenty years, and never missed but one Sunday's service in all that time; and at a school where he taught for the same number of years, he was equally regular in attendance. Both my parents inculcated a love of order and punctuality, with industry; and their children have all proved the advantage of this teaching. My beloved mother ever impressed upon us that talent, without perseverance in application and steadiness in diligence and assiduity, was of small practical avail. Example constantly seconded precept in all her wise lessons; and this made them be taken into the hearts as well as the minds of her children.

The more I look at the charming little daguerreotype figure the more I admire it. It is so beautifully simple in attitude, so easy in dress, so unaffected and unstudied, so Shakespearean, in short. The droop of the head, thoughtful and reposeful, bringing into prominence the broad expansive forehead, suggests intellectual supremacy better than all the upturned looks and eyes cast to heaven that were

ever invented by the Frenchy imagination of a
Roubiliac[1] to represent ideality. Poetic reverie
does not take a displayful and commonplace air.
When William Shakespeare wrote his great
creations, we do not fancy him holding a pencil
to his brow after the manner of a melodramatic
actor. In the lovely little portrait of him that
now lies open before me, we may picture him to
ourselves as just pausing in one of his field
strolls around green Stratford-on-Avon, and
pondering some suddenly-conceived thought, or
fresh-imagined scene. The very closure of the
hands has eloquence in it. I thank you very
warmly for this valuable gift, dear sir, and assure
you it will be highly prized and carefully treasured by me, for its own sake, as well as for that
of its kind giver. Tell the artist, if ever he
fulfil his hope of becoming a tragic actor, I
should like to play the part of the Nurse to his
Romeo, for the pleasure of enacting Shakespeare
with one who has so well embodied the poet's
own figure.

---

[1] Louis François Roubiliac. Died 1762. A French sculptor,
much better known in England than in his own country.

OCT. 9TH, 1856,
27 PORCHESTER TERRACE, BAYSWATER.

.   .   .   .

CHARLES and I went together last Saturday to take leave of dear and honoured Leigh Hunt, at his cottage in Hammersmith. We had a charming two hours with him. His dear beautiful poet-face looked as fine in its faded thinness as it used to in its smooth and rounded manhood, when I first beheld it, years ago. His glorious eyes were softened, not dimmed; and they filled with as bright drops of enthusiasm, while we talked of the immortal things in this world, — Poetry and Love, — as they ever did. Those handsome locks, once black as a raven's wing, now white and sparer, still hung round the bland countenance with a grace which hardly any man's hair I ever saw can boast in a like degree. The old tenderness of smile, the old lighting of the eyes, the old witchery of words and manner were all there, touched into a something nobler and thoughtfuller than formerly. I felt the old worship in me which as a girl moved me to romance of admiration toward him that few could imagine in this soberer age, when I raised one of his hands to my lips, while Charles clasped the other. That moment, when thus linked between two men so

[254]

pre-eminently objects of my homage, will often and oftener recur to my memory hereafter, as among the proudest instants of my life.

Your affectionate

MARY COWDEN CLARKE.

MAISON QUAGLIA AU PORT, NICE, SARDINIA,
NOVEMBER 12, 1856.

MY DEAR ENTHUSIAST:

YOUR little note of the 30th Sept., accompanied by Mrs. Balmanno's kind letter announcing her beautiful present to me, arrived the very last thing before I left dear old England. The post brought it to me on the morning of our departure, and it was the final crown of all my long train of pleasant communications in the beloved home place. Since we have been here, Alf has made two pleasant excursions into the neighbouring mountains, which are of great height and beauty, some wild and bare, others cultivated, and crowned with sequestered villages. The first time I declined being of the party, as mule-back formed one of its features, and I feared my strength might prove inadequate and make me a hindrance to the others; but the second time I accompanied them, and very much I enjoyed it. We — Sabilla, Alfred,

[255]

Charles, and myself — set off in an open carriage after an early breakfast here, along a road which winds up the valley, gradually ascending all the way towards the mountains. At a little hamlet on the brink of a torrent river called the Vesuvio, we quitted the carriage and commenced ascending a steep mountain path, which led to a small village named Utelle, where Alf proposed we should sleep. Anything more primitive and secluded than this perched-up mountain village you can hardly imagine. A faint early moon scarcely sufficed, amid the gathering shades of evening, to show that we had arrived (after a toilsome climb of about an hour and a half) in a miniature rubble-paved square, dignified by the name of La Place, where some goats, cows, and sheep were watering at a rude fountain, together with a mule or two and a few loitering inhabitants of the spot, who seemed scarcely less animal than the cattle, and who stared at us as if we had dropped from some neighbouring planet. We accosted one of these half-human beings, and asked him (in the country patois, which Sabilla contrives to speak and understand, for the people hereabouts do not talk French nor Italian, but a mongrel dialect composed of both) to show us the inn. He proved to be the landlord of the only house bearing any pretensions to the character of a hostelry; and, after asking us what on earth could have brought us to that spot, he led us into a rough building, looking something between a granary and a hovel. We groped along a dark passage, blundered up some stone steps flanked by huge, worm-eaten, wooden banisters, and found ourselves in a room bare of all articles of furniture save a clumsy table and chairs, a wooden clothes-press, and a side-ledge, on which lay two or three packs of dirty cards and some piles of woollen cloth. We had, providently, brought our own tea; so some boiling water, and milk, with a loaf whose hardness announced at least a week's previous baking, made us a welcome meal. Our sleeping-rooms were in the same style of primitive bareness; the one in which Sabilla and I slept (for we had only two bedrooms between our party, and the landlord, with his characteristic frankness, told us we might think ourselves lucky to get those) seemed like a nook sliced off from a loft, and reminded me of some of the chambers mentioned in "Don Quixote" as occupied for sleeping-apartments by Sancho and his master, at the inns where they sojourned. Sleep was out of the question for me, I was so intensely haunted by a sense of height and isolation, of being hung up as it were mid-air; but morning sunshine revived me, and we set forth to a beautiful little chapel, dedicated to the Virgin and perched on a rocky eminence still farther up the mountain, on its very apex, and which commanded one of the grandest views I ever beheld in my life. The legend attached to this little sanctuary increases its interest. It is said to have been built by a poor mariner in danger of shipwreck, who vowed, if he were saved from peril, to erect a chapel dedicated to the Virgin, on a height that could command a view of the sea nearest to his native village. Altogether we enjoyed our mountain trip greatly. The weather has been beautifully warm and fine since we have been here, and the month is November.

My space only allows me to subscribe myself, which I do in all affection and sincerity, your

M. C. C.

MAISON QUAGLIA AU PORT, NICE, SARDINIA,
JULY 12, 1857.

MY DEAR ENTHUSIAST:

I ENCLOSE you a letter for my brother Alfred, as you will know where he is, and either forward it to him or keep it for him, according to your own judgment.

My Charles had a delightful letter from dear Leigh Hunt by yesterday's post, in reply to one

[258]

wherein Charles told him that he had requested the publishers to send him a copy of "World-noted Women" when it should appear; and also mentioned the intended edition of Shakespeare as having been confided to my hands. I transcribe for you Leigh Hunt's own pleasant words, as they will both please your father-in-love's partiality and will make you smile. He says : " I long to see the Fifteen Famous Women, and am truly obliged by the desire expressed to the publishers to send it to me. It is impossible they could be in better hands than in those of the bringing up of the women of Shakespeare, — people that make a Mormon of me, and (with your leave) a Molly of me, as well as Polygamist. Indeed, with the help of another *l*, the latter word might express both." And afterwards he says : " I must not omit to congratulate you both, and everybody else, on the new edition of Shakespeare, especially as I reckon upon her turning her unique knowledge of him to dainty account in her Preface." Enchanting as it is to have such kind words of encouragement from dear Leigh Hunt, you must know, my dear sir, they half frighten me, as they show what he expects; and while the limited time in which I was compelled to execute my task with regard to the " World-noted Women " makes me feel that they are not so amply done as they might have been had they not been finished within so short a space, I have still more secret dreads and doubts lest I should never be able to put down all that is in my head on the other and far greater subject. However, my whole soul and endeavour shall be brought to the task; *that* you may be sure of. I think of nothing else, I read hardly anything else, I ponder and re-ponder it over and over, again and again. The letter from dear Leigh Hunt is full of beautiful things, grave and gay, quite his own fine, thoughtful, yet serene philosophy. It is delightful to see a poet, a genius, like him, so fresh and vigorous, so young in spirit and feeling throughout. He writes as energetically and charmingly now as ever, and you know what an admirable gift he always possessed in the epistolary way. His letters, like his talk, are perfection. Have you heard of the edition of his works that is coming out in America? He has promised that we shall have a copy. You must know that that is my especial delight, presentation copies of books from their Authors. I prize those I possess, beyond all my other treasures. I cherish a certain copy of " Bleak House," wherein is written " Mary Cowden Clarke, with the regards of Charles Dickens," like a jewel inestimable; and no sum could represent the amount of value I set upon a little volume containing the Caudle Lectures, bearing the playful inscription, " Presented with great timidity but equal regard, to Mrs. Cowden Clarke by Douglas Jerrold." Ah, my dear sir, what a cruel loss is there! to us, to all! God bless you.

MARY COWDEN CLARKE.

NICE, JULY 31ST, 1857.

MY DEAR ENTHUSIAST:

THIS last week has brought me your kind and delightful letter of the 10th (arrived here the 27th) announcing the welcome news of dear Alf's safe arrival in New York. Your description of meeting him, and finding him a regular John Bull, etc., all enchanted me; I was so glad to have a minute account of it all. Your account of kissing Harriet Beecher Stowe's hand interested me greatly and made me long that I could have done the same thing. It was a noble hand, and fearlessly set down what the heart's indignation prompted, bearing honest and eloquent testimony against crying evil. Besides your dear and welcome letter, this week brought me Alf's journal on board ship, which he kindly kept for the behoof of his sisters. Clara and

Sabilla forwarded it on to me here, much to Charles's and my enjoyment. There is to be quite a family gathering just now at that enchanting Devonshire park. Cecilia, Clara, and Sabilla are going down for a few days during the summer holidays to see dear Aunt Catherine at Ugbrooke. You may be sure my heart will be with them; yet a bit of it is in America!

Ever your affectionate

M. C. C.

NICE, AUG. 28, 1857.

MY DEAR ENTHUSIAST:

AGAIN I request your kind offices by the enclosed note, in giving it, or forwarding it, to my brother. Charles and I have been much gratified in reading aloud — he reading to me, while I work — the life of Shakespeare by Thomas Campbell. It is put together in a most pleasant spirit, which all the biographies are not. But a poet is sure to write well on a poet. Everything that Coleridge, for instance, says of our Idol is in charming taste; and also Barry Cornwall's Memoir and Essay on Shakespeare and his Writings, has the same delightful poetic charm. After reading the heap of inappreciative discussion on the subject, it is truly refreshing to go through the dissertations of such authors as these, upon our poet of poets. They can best feel his merits, and can therefore most veneratingly and modestly treat the theme of his genius and greatness.

With united kindest regards from Charles and myself to you and Mrs. Balmanno, believe me to be

Gratefully,

MARY COWDEN CLARKE.

MAISON QUAGLIA AU PORT, NICE, SARDINIA,
JAN. 28, 1858.

MY DEAR ENTHUSIAST:

IT seems an age since I have either heard from or written to you. I am the greater delinquent, since I did receive from you a little note dated November 3rd, which I have allowed to remain unacknowledged all this time. But somehow or other, what with Christmas, and the New Year, and Clara's sudden going to England for the Princess Royal's marriage, etc., the weeks have flown by unwittingly.

A kind friend lately sent us over here some good notices of "World-noted Women;" and Charles and I were so much pleased with the excellent style of the writing as well as the laudatory tone of the article in the "Glasgow

[263]

Citizen," and of that in the " Northampton Mercury," that we have requested copies to be sent of each of these papers to yourself and to the Messrs. Appleton. This, dear sir, and father-in-love, is yet another gratification of the kind I owe to you.

> " One ' glory ' to another still succeeds,
>   Another and another after that,
>   And the last ' fame ' is as welcome as the former."

Clara and her husband are gone over to England for the grand state occasion of the Princess Royal's marriage.[1] They did intend to have remained the whole of the winter at Nice this year; but so flatteringly strong a desire was expressed at Court for Clara's presence, that she made all other views give way to the pleasure of gratifying the Queen, who has always been graciousness itself to dear Clara, both as woman and as artist. In Clara's case, Her Majesty seems to have taken particular pleasure in marking her estimation of good character and ladylike conduct, as well as of pre-eminent artistic talent.

I ought to tell you of a little comedietta which we got up here, to greet the return of the children's parents, and their Uncle Alfred and Aunt

---

[1] Victoria Adelaide Mary Louisa married to Prince Frederick William, Crown Prince of Germany, Jan. 25, 1858, and afterwards known as Empress Queen Frederick of Germany.

Sabilla. I wrote this juvenile drama for the little Italians — partly as a good exercise for them in English-speaking, partly for their entertainment and enjoyment. It was called " The Godmother," and was enacted by Giovanni, Portia, Mario, and Valeria Gigliucci, and by my husband and myself. The scene was laid in a drawing-room; the characters were simple, the plot was not intricate, and the dialogue was suited to the several performers' powers. Our audience consisted of Count Gigliucci, Alfred, Sabilla, in the front seats; our women-servants, and our cook's husband in the back row. The latter was highly amused, and particularly struck with the godmother's (played by your daughter-in-love) costume; which consisted of patched clothes as a disguise, and of a full-dress beneath, ornamented with jewels — which appeared in the last scene, when the disguise was thrown off. Clara was our prompter and stage-manager, and she it was who drilled the chicks in their parts. She also played an overture previous to the performance in the shape of a duetto on the pianoforte, executed by her eldest girl, Portia, and herself. I must not omit to mention a little incident that struck me very delightfully, and will, I think, interest you. When Clara came forward to play this musical piece with her little daughter, and they curtseyed to the rapturous applause with which the audience received them, I saw Clara turn as red as a rose. She, who has faced her audiences by thousands and tens of thousands, — she who had just come from singing at the Handel Festival in the Crystal Palace, — she actually blushed, up to her very temples, as she met the applause of her husband, brother, and sisters. I cannot tell you, my dear sir, how pleasantly this little circumstance touched me; it showed thoroughly how completely a public life leaves a really fine nature unspoiled and unhackneyed in feeling.

After the little play we had a repast of cakes, fruit, and sweetmeats, for the delectation of the distinguished performers; and I assure you, they, with their elders among both the company and audience, enjoyed and did ample justice to the banquet. In short, the whole thing went off brilliantly, and it was agreed on all hands that the entertainment was a complete success.

Our whole family circle join in kindest compliments and best wishes of the season to yourself and Mrs. Balmanno. From myself, dear sir, accept my ever grateful affection.

MARY COWDEN CLARKE.

NICE, FEB. 21ST, 1858.

MY DEAR ENTHUSIAST:

WE have been quite gay — for us, wonderfully — of late. Clara and her husband arrived from England well and happy; and on the morning of their arrival, their four children got up a concert to greet them. It was quite a grand affair. We had the chairs ranged in order in our drawing-room, and the pianoforte drawn out, so as to look as much like a real concert-room as possible; and then the four young "distinguished Italian artists" played their pieces in succession. There was, as you may believe, great applause; for the audience consisted of father, mother, uncles, and aunts. Afterwards we had a carriage, and sallied forth to witness the Carnival, which was then at its height. All Nice was out on the Corso. Every window was occupied with gazers; every balcony was thronged with people. There was a carriage-way preserved by gens d'armes mounted on horseback; while the pedestrians lined the footways, and sitters occupied the fronts of the houses. Every one threw, threw, threw! Bouquets of flowers, sugarplums of colored chalk showered in the air. Nothing but pelting went on. It was well we were provided with wire masks, or our faces would have suffered. The more you are thrown at, the more distinguished you are; and our carriage was so much favoured, that on arriving at home its floor was heaped with sugarplums and nosegays. We were supplied with two huge basketfuls of bouquets, and each of us had an apron with a capacious pocket like a turnpike man's, filled with bonbons; so that we were nowise behindhand in our return of complimentary throwings. A perfect hail of sugarplums darkened the air; showers of bouquets were hurled hither and thither; all was uproar, laughter, and merry confusion. It was a sight to see; and I was very glad to have witnessed it. Another sister of mine, Cecilia (Mrs. Serle), is staying with us at present on a visit, by my brother's invitation. Her youngest child is in delicate health, and being ordered change of air and sea-bathing, Alfred asked Cecilia to bring little Lydia, and spend some time at Nice. They are enjoying themselves very much; and the Carnival happened in timely occasion to heighten their amusement.

Clara brought me from England several pleasant letters from friends; among others a charming letter from dear Leigh Hunt, in which he speaks of having just written to New York, to thank the Messrs. Appleton for sending him a copy of their handsome work, "World-Noted

Women." I daresay my kind Enthusiast will manage to promise his daughter-in-love a sight of dear Leigh Hunt's letter, as he did that of Miss F. Nightingale. Charles and I have been delighted with a poem (of which L. H. has sent us a manuscript copy) that has lately appeared in Fraser's Magazine, entitled "The Tapiser's Tale; attempted in the manner of Chaucer, by Leigh Hunt." Do you see Fraser? And have you seen this admirable " Tapiser's Tale "? If not, pray do; I am sure you will be delighted with it. With lovingest wishes for you and yours,

MARY COWDEN CLARKE.

NICE, APRIL 28, 1858.

MY DEAR ENTHUSIAST:

I HAVE to acknowledge the receipt of three delightful letters from you. I should feel even more remorse than I do at having left them so long unacknowledged, were it not that Alfred has done so for me, in a measure, by explaining to you how closely my time is now engaged upon our Idol. Ever since Dyce has arrived I have been giving hourly attention to the text, comparing all the editions, going through the whole regularly; and with a care and diligence that remind me of the old Concordance days. Charles and I are up before five every morning, work till breakfast, return to writing immediately after, never leave it till an hour before dinner (at six o'clock), take our air-and-exercise walk; and in the evening I transcribe the result of my day's labour, so as to have a correct duplicate copy, by which I may be able to check the proofs at the last. . . .

29TH. Dear Clara and her husband left for England yesterday. Charles and I therefore look forward to another year of Darby-and-Joaning it together. Shakespeare and mutual love make the time pass happily, and console us for giving up all holidays. I think Alfred told you that we gave up already a charming excursion. The party — consisting of Alfred and his three sisters, Cecilia, Clara, and Sabilla — came back in raptures with their tour. One of its incidents was very interesting. Among the places Alfred planned to take in their way and visit, was a spot called Novello, a mere village now, but formerly a place of some seigneurial importance; very picturesquely situated, and containing an old mansion-house, somewhat in the Radcliffian-castle style. They were wandering about, looking at the edifice and noting the arms in escutcheon over the door, observing that they in all material particulars corresponded with the "old coat"

found at Venice for us by the Herald-office there
some time since, — the ancient shield of the Novello family, — when an old gentleman accosted
our party, and seeing them interested, told them
a host of particulars relative to the place: how
the house had been a seat of the Novello family,
how the arms were theirs, how he himself was a
kind of descendant, etc. He went on to say that
the last Novello, being a female, had married the
Marquis de Rora, and thus the possession had
passed out of the family; that having no offspring
the name had died out, and," added he, looking
straight at Alfred, "there are now no Novellos
left." When he found out who the party were,
he was in his turn greatly interested, showed
them every hospitality, gave them some wine
grown on and made on the estate, took them
over the old house, showed them the family pictures, etc. They parted mutually pleased with
each other, and with the understanding that the
old gentleman was to let Alfred know the sum
for which the estate was to be purchased. It
would have been a curious thing if Alf had become its ultimate possessor. It would have been
quite a modern realization of an old romance —
the long-lost rightful heir coming into his seigneurial possession! But it seems that — apart
from the pleasant fancy — the climate is not

genial in the winter. The sight and views are fine in the extreme; but the position renders the spot bleak and subject to cold winds and frosts. Novello will be an enchanting spot to visit, and to dote upon in imagination, but not to become lord of.

The weather here is now beautiful, warm without being too hot. The winter visitors are all departing, but for a month or two longer Nice will be very enjoyable. As the heat increases, we shall guard against its overpowering us, by the same precaution we took last year; and thus, I trust, be able to persevere in our close, hard work until it be completed. Even I, who know Shakespeare with the knowledge of long attachment, had no idea of the immense labour editing his works would prove. The conscientious consideration necessary for each disputed reading is almost incalculable; no one who has not gone through the task would believe. For no other writer could one take the enormous pains required. I, in my anxious scrupulousness, — which makes Charles laugh at me heartily and perpetually, — am perfectly haunted by my debatable bits; they flavour my every meal; I taste them in every morsel I eat; I cogitate them in my walks; I dream of them in my sleep; I have a besetting notion of their presence; they "dog me like my murderer;"[1] "fears and scruples shake us,"[2] as I ponder over the various suggested lections. When I have been silent some time and Charles asks me a sudden question, I start from my trance, and answer some wild, incoherent words, that prove to be a conglomeration of the different proposed alterations of some perplexing passage. Seriously, however, the typographical and transcribing errors of that First Folio give rise to most anxious canvassing in the mind of any one who undertakes to tread their labyrinth in order to ascertain and decide the probable text of the author. Fortunately, he is fully worth any amount of pains taken for him; and the delight of re-reading and re-considering him amply counterbalances the fatigue and solicitude. For the thousandth time Charles and I revel in his beauties, while plodding through his difficulties, or rather, those of his printers and transcribers.

With affectionate greetings from us all to yourself and Mrs. Balmanno.

MARY COWDEN CLARKE.

---

[1] " I have dogged him like his murderer." — " Twelfth Night," Act III, Scene II.

[2] "Macbeth," Act II, Scene III.

NICE, JUNE 28, 1858.

MY DEAR ENTHUSIAST:

I HAVE to thank you for your kind letter of May 6th; which has remained thus shamefully unacknowledged because I have been so closely and constantly at work upon Our Edition that I have had no moment for anything else. Your welcome communication arrived just as we were stepping into a carriage that Alf had engaged to take us out for an evening drive, that we might enjoy the fresh air and gentle exercise after working hard all day from dawn. These evening drives that he contrived for us were most charming, and doubly valuable to Charles and myself, coming as they did "between lights," at a time when we could not see to write. On the evening your letter arrived, we went to a lovely spot about two miles from here, called the Val St. Andre. It is a beautiful valley, nestled amid grand crags of rock. At the entrance there is a castle and a chapel picturesquely situated at the mouth of the glen, along which are rows of cypress trees and tufted underwood. In the bed of the torrent there is a brawling stream, which proceeds from a cavernous grotto hung with ferns and adiantums, and which tumbles and sparkles — a silver cascade of water that drops from a considerable height. On the even-

[274]

ing in question, the dear little nightingales —
who abound in this glen — first made themselves heard for the season, and regaled my
ears, while Alf, reminded by the advent of your
letter, repeated to us the incidents of his
pleasant evening drive with you and Mrs. Balmanno, and recalled many particulars of his
delightful American visit, as we drove leisurely
through the beautiful Italian valley. We enjoyed
reading your letter as we went along, and bade
Pasquale — our driver — proceed slowly, that we
might do so.

You ask me if I know what portrait that could
be of dear Charles Lamb, a full-length. I know
of none such, save the little etching which appears in a second volume of his "Letters,"
edited by Talfourd, and published by Moxon in
1837. It gives a fair idea — somewhat exagger-
ated — of his general appearance, for he was
thin to attenuation; but the portrait by Wageman — the frontispiece to the same volume —
is an excellent likeness of his honoured face.

With kindest regards to Mrs. Balmanno, believe me your affectionate

M. C. C.

AUG. 15, 1858.

MY DEAR ENTHUSIAST:

SINCE I have heard the news that the Atlantic Telegraph is completed, I have been longing to write to you in mutual congratulation upon an event which we both must feel to be so grand a one in its future effects upon the two great nations which it unites. Is it not a fine realization of our Idol's idea of "putting a girdle round about the earth in forty minutes"? It makes Master Puck himself slow!

SEPT. 22. Huza-a-a-a-a-a-a-a-h! We have this day sent off *the* edition of Shakespeare. It was finished yesterday; and we immediately packed it up, and took it ourselves to the diligence office, at the other end of the town. You should have seen Charles's beautiful packing; the parcel was a perfect picture of its kind. However, when we presented it at the so-called diligence office, the clerk looked as if we had offered him a treasonous fardel containing a condensation of combustible complots that would blow up all France as they passed through that unhappy, tindery land. He first informed us that we must make a declaration of what the parcel contained; and when we cheerfully complied, in the full confidence that our reply must be satisfactory, saying, "Books — only books,"

[276]

he started, as if his worst fears were confirmed, and said in a horror-stricken tone, " Ah! books! they are forbidden to enter France." "Oh, well, but Shakespeare, Shakespeare," we exclaimed, "he is of course an exception; he passes free everywhere; the most barbarous countries make an exception in his favour, and understand that he may be admitted everywhere." The clerk shook his head, and assured us that we were quite mistaken; and we found that though savages comprehend that Shakespeare has liberty to pass wherever he pleases, enlightened France has not arrived at that conclusion. Or rather I should say, the cunning despot[1] whom France permits to lead her by the nose and set his heel on her brain, has sufficient discernment to perceive that the exclusion of knowledge from the territory he domineers over is one way to prolong his hour of power. You may conceive our dismay, when we found ourselves thus disappointed of conveying the parcel by coach, or diligence, as they style it; which always makes one remember Jonathan Oldbuck's[2] broadside of reproaches against the diligence and the old hag it belongs to! "Diligence, quoth 'a? Thou shouldst have

[1] Napoleon III.
[2] " The Antiquary." Walter Scott.

[277]

called it the sloth!" Well, we bethought ourselves of the liberal compact between advanced
Sardinia and blessed England in postal arrangement; and accordingly, having repacked the
parcel, separating the printed and the manuscript portions and making them up into ap-
pointedly arranged packets for transmission, we
took them this morning early to the post office;
and on the prepayment of about one pound
twelve shillings and sixpence in English money,
sent off our completed work. Once more, I say
Huzz a-a-a-a-a-ah! and I hear your hearty echo,
across the Atlantic.

With my Charles's and my own kindest regards to yourself and dear Mrs. Balmanno,
believe me to be

Your obliged
MARY COWDEN CLARKE.

NICE, DEC. 5TH, 1858.

MY DEAR ENTHUSIAST:

I AM delighted to have it in my power to send
you the precious gem you want; a letter of
dear and honoured Charles Lamb's. Among the
few we possess, the enclosed is almost the only
one which possesses his signature at full length.
He generally only subscribed "C. L." This is
in every respect peculiarly valuable, as you will

perceive; but I have the greater pleasure in giving it to *you*, my dear father-in-love who have been so affectionately generous to the daughter of her to whom it is addressed; and that you should be thus enabled to oblige a friend who you say has been so kindly influential on your behalf, gives me gratification indeed.

DEC. 10TH. This has in vain been delayed, under the hope that I might be able to mention the arrival of a letter. As a relaxation after my hard work, my kind men-folk have taken me very frequently to see an excellent Italian company of actors, now performing here. They play at a small theatre; but their acting is delightful. One among them especially is an admirable comedian; he reminds Charles and me of the days of Munden, Dowton, and Liston. His name is Giovanni Toselli; and he combines in a masterly degree humour, ease, good byplay, varied gesture, high spirits, vivacity, earnestness, and an extraordinary versatility and power of individual impersonation. We go whenever he plays, he is so superexcellent. Alfred has also taken a box at the opera for the season; but I seldom go, as the modern style of music does not greatly please my taste. Charles has commenced another series of drawing-room lectures to our circle of acquaintance here, and as usual there is an anxiety to

procure invitations that causes quite an excitement in this quiet little place. Alfred was compelled to order a large number of new chairs, in
order to accommodate our immensely increased
assemblage. We are quite amused at the interest excited; but it is gratifying too, particularly
to the lecturer's wife. I shall be looking forward
to the pleasure of hearing from you as soon after
the receipt of this as you feel inclined to write,
that I may know dear Charles Lamb's letter has
reached you safely.

   With our united kindest regards to you and
Mrs. Balmanno, believe me,
                           Gratefully,
                              MARY COWDEN CLARKE.

* * *

                              NICE, DEC. 25, 1858.
MY DEAR ENTHUSIAST:

YOUR welcome note of the 29th November,
    enclosed in one to my brother, came as a
delightful Christmas greeting this morning at
breakfast time; and I sit down at once to answer
and thank you for it. You will, I trust, ere this,
have safely received my last, dated Dec. 5th and
10th (containing a note of dear and honoured
Charles Lamb's), in reply to your kind communication of the 16th November, sending me vari-

ous Shakespearian items, for which many, many thanks. I have a small pencil-portrait of Leigh Hunt in our copy of his " Rimini," which was drawn by Anne Gliddon at the request of my beloved mother, who wished to encourage the young artist by an ordered picture.

The clever Italian company of actors which I mentioned to you in my last has, alas, taken its departure. We quite miss the resource which Toselli's admirable performance afforded us; and here, where there is a perfect dearth of any entertainment, the loss is no slight one to Charles and myself. On the farewell night we mustered a large family party to take leave ; and Clara and I took down to the theatre a parting gift each which we had prepared for Toselli's child, a little daughter. Clara's was a box of bon-bons ; mine a doll, dressed by myself. You and Mrs. Balmanno would have laughed, could you have seen the pains it cost me to array Miss Dolly in her suit of pink satin and pink crêpe, with turquoise ornaments, and hair dressed with roses and lilies of the valley. A basket of flowers was borne in her hand, attached to which was a scroll in Italian, bidding adieu to the excellent dramatic company. The packet containing the doll was inscribed with a few words, also in Italian, importing that it was a gift to the little daughter of Giovanni Toselli, from a sincere admirer of his pre-eminent talent. Fortunately we had an opportunity of presenting our offerings to the father himself, who chanced to be at the door when we entered; and you should have seen his bright eyes glisten and his expressive mouth quiver, when Clara and I advanced and delivered our packets into his hand, with words of remembrance to his pretty, clever little girl, who had played a small part in one of the pieces one evening. We hear the company is gone to play near Genoa; and Charles and I had a pleasant idea of going there for a few days and taking Toselli by surprise at finding us in our old seat in the stalls, on the opening night there; but this, like many other pleasant schemes, vanished into air, with several of our favourite castles which I possess in that region.

To both you and herself, scores of kind wishes of the season, Christmas and New Year's greetings are sent from all the family assembled here. Accept them, as they are offered, heartily and sincerely, and believe that no one more thoroughly (as there is no one who has such strong cause) offers them to you than

MARY COWDEN CLARKE.

FEB. 8, 1859.

MY DEAR ENTHUSIAST:

I HAVE the pleasure of informing you that we this day send off the first batch of proofs of our edition of Shakespeare. Alfred and Sabilla are gone for a week or two to Genoa. The weather is dull and overcast at present here; but I trust they may be more fortunate where they are.

Dear Leigh Hunt is writing a series of articles in the Spectator just now, with all his native spirit. Do you see them? If not, I am sure you would be delighted to read one he lately wrote upon the Burns Commemoration. In the course of it he gives an admirable song which he has written to the measure of the old Scottish reel-tune of Tullochgorum, to which you have doubtless danced many a time! I will copy out the song for you, as I know you will like to read it, and to see how finely our admired Leigh Hunt retains his fire and animation of style.

BURNS AND TULLOCHGORUM

Come let us have a dance, and make
The mirth complete for Burns's sake,
For how can feet not long to take
The steps he took before 'em?
Who can keep them ever still,

Who can keep, who can keep them,
Who can keep them ever still,
When strong the will comes o'er 'em?
Who can keep them ever still,
When song itself shall urge the will,
And music grind like any mill
The reel of Tullochgorum?
" O Tullochgorum 's my delight,"
Said Burns's fine old herald, hight
The Reverend Mr. Skinner, wight
That hated false decorum:
It was his and Burns's too,
His and Burns's, his and Burns's,
It was his and Burns's too,
And all such true *virorum*:
It was his and Burns's too,
And doubly thus becomes his due
From all that ever shake a shoe
At sound of Tullochgorum.
For Tullochgorum 's such a dance,
As never yet was found in France,
Though some French dames, whose sons could prance,
To Scottish husbands bore 'em:
Mirth it has and muscle both,
Mirth and muscle, mirth and muscle,
Mirth it has and muscle both,
And graces *angelorum*:
Mirth it has and muscle both,
And makes all friends, as Skinner show'th:
Quakers themselves would take an oath,
There 's naught like Tullochgorum.
'T was in this dance, there 's not a doubt,
The poet's Jean first turned about
His heart, when footing in and out,
Her charms made eyes adore 'em:
She was a singing, dancing jade,
Singing, dancing, singing, dancing,

> She was a singing, dancing jade,
> And full of grace *flexorum :* [1]
> She was a singing, dancing jade,
> And naught beside; so Envy said;
> But capital goodwife she made
> Inspired by Tullochgorum.
> Who better could have played his part,
> In such a dance, than he whose art
> Of pleasing was all life and heart,
> And no fatigue could floor 'em?
> Think, lads and lasses, how he bade,
> Lads and lasses, lads and lasses,
> Think, lads and lasses, how he bade
> Your loves all truthward soar 'em:
> Think how he made kind natures glad,
> And only brutes and bigots sad,
> Then if you can, don't dance like mad
> The reel of Tullochgorum.

You ask me, my dear sir, whether I can read your writing on that thin paper. Beautifully, I assure you. I only hope you can make out my small scribble half as well. Give my husband's and my own united love to your dear wife, and accept the same yourself, believing me always to be

>   Your affectionate daughter-in-love
>   (What a pretty title that was you invented!)
>   MARY COWDEN CLARKE.

---

[1] The muscles to-wit, called — in anatomical Latin and in the nominative case — "flexores," or benders. — L. H.

MY DEAR ENTHUSIAST:

I FEAR you will think me very remiss in having thus long deferred acknowledging your kind letters. I have been prevented by a serious accident I met with, which kept me in bed and unable to work for many days. Charles had accompanied Sabilla and the Gigliuccis to the opera one evening (Alfred having been called to England by business which required his presence in London), contrary to his usual custom of going out without me. But I had wished to stay at home and look at my new batch of Shakespeare proofs, which had arrived by post the day before. Finding my candles burning low, I called to Miette to change them; but spoke not loud for fear of awakening my father, whose sleeping-room is near to mine. Advancing to the staircase — of stone, like all stairs here — I went down the first short flight, and thought I had reached the landing; but I missed the last step, fell forward, lost my balance, and plunged headlong down the lower flight of fifteen stairs. The servants, terrified at the noise, rushed out, to find me lying in a heap and streaming with blood from a deep wound in my head. They raised me, supported me into the parlour, and laid me on the sofa, while they sent for a surgeon. I could not help casting rueful looks at my thumb, — fortunately the left, — which was horribly awry, in fact, dislocated. But my chief care was to try my brain, as it were to see if I could think. I found I was perfectly collected and remembered all that had happened and all that was to be done. I gave strict injunctions that the news be broken carefully, on the return of Charles and Sabilla; that all traces of the accident should be cleared away before they came back; that some one should go upstairs and see to the papers and candle I had left burning; and that some warm water should be brought, — into which I plunged my distorted thumb, and held it there, that it might keep supple until the surgeon came to set it. That was excruciating pain; but for the honour of old England I bore it bravely and received the compliments of the surgeon on my courage. Fortunately, my husband and sister were spared witnessing this torture, for the thumb was just set when they returned. But, poor things, they were sufficiently startled, as you may suppose, when they were met at the carriage door by our cook's husband, who told them by degrees that an accident had occurred to madame; and they came up to find me lying on the bed surrounded by the servants, while the surgeon was dressing the wound near my temple. Charles says the first thing that calmed his alarm was my voice, saying in a firm quiet tone, " It's nothing; it's nothing; don't be afraid, dears." Although frightful to witness (my clothes saturated with blood), yet this free flow saved me from fever; and there was no need to use the lancet. My surgeon was kind and clever; and my sister Sabilla has been a Dr. Elizabeth Blackwell and a Florence Nightingale in one, throughout.

One curious circumstance occurred, which I must tell you. I had told Marianne — our excellent cook-servant, who has been with us for more than nine years, and is more a friend than a dependant — to draw off my Shakespeare seal-ring, lest the hand should swell, being much bruised. She did not notice that the stone was gone (so violent was my fall, that the gold setting was battered in, and the stone forced out); and it was four days before the loss was discovered. I learned that the sawdust, strewn to obliterate the traces of the accident on the stairs, as I had directed, had been swept away and carried to the dust heap in the grounds, at some little distance from the house. The fear was that the peasants had already scattered this dust heap, which they use for manure. However, I caused it to be notified that a sum of money would be the reward of whoever might be the fortunate finder of the dark little stone, whose size, shape, colour, and engraved seal-head I minutely described. You perhaps know what peculiar cause I have to prize that ring, it having been my beloved mother's gift, to commemorate the completion of the Concordance, and can readily imagine my anxiety to recover it. A busy search of two hours, in which both peasants and servants joined, resulted in the dear little Shakespeare seal being found by the lad employed by the chief peasant. I was especially glad he was the finder, for it seems he had run for the surgeon, run to the chemist for drugs, and, in short, made himself generally useful on the night of the accident; and I heard that he was so rejoiced at his good fortune that he sang, danced, and skipped about during two whole days after I had sent him the promised reward. He told our Miette that he would willingly, at any time of the night or the day (for he had got up out of his warm bed to run for the doctor that night, these peasants go to bed so early), and run anywhere to do any service for madame. The kindly zeal shown me by every one in this late affair, — by Marianne, who sat up with me the first night; by her husband, who lifted me from the ground and supported me into the parlour, and afterwards upstairs to my own room; by Miette, the pretty housemaid, who held the light for the surgeon, and who hails my recovery with daily smiles of pleasure and congratulation; by the very peasants in the grounds, — all prove how kindly is the attachment inspired by sympathy and interest evinced in their concerns at other times. The substantial good done for Marianne, her husband, and children, by our beloved mother; the occasional ribbons and smarteries bestowed upon Miette, together with counsel about sweethearts, and reading and writing lessons from Charles and myself; the bon-bons I keep in my pocket for the behoof of the children of the peasants, and the constant "bon-jours" we exchange with their parents as we pass through the grounds, make them regard us with a kindliness that is felt to be very precious in a time of trouble; and I assure you, my dear sir, among the many sources of gratitude your daughter-in-love has had to acknowledge with heartfelt thankfulness to God lately, — who permitted her accident to have so few serious consequences when it might have had such fatal ones, — has certainly been the affectionate attention she has met with from all around her.

Before Alf went to England, he had talked
of a little spring tour together in the south of
France, as change of air and scene would be
beneficial for Charles and me; now it would
be more advisable than ever. Therefore it is
probable Sabilla, Charles, and myself may meet
him at Avignon in May, and take a short excursion together to see Nismes, Arles, Vaucluse,
and, if possible, snatch a glimpse of Pyrenean
scenery; after which he and Sabilla repair to
England for the Handel Festival, while Charles
and I return to Nice and Shakespeare-proofs.
We shall see how my wounded cranium and
helpless thumb will permit the carrying out of
this pleasant plan. My wounded head does not
allow me to apply long at a time to writing;
therefore I know you will forgive and continue
to indulge

MARY COWDEN CLARKE.

Our joint kindest regards and remembrances
to Mrs. Balmanno, with hearty admiration of
her charming volume.

AUG. 7, 1859, NICE.

MY DEAR ENTHUSIAST:

WE have enjoyed a great treat, Charles
reading aloud to me while I worked in
the perusal of a new work on Shakespeare, which

I daresay you have seen announced. Directly we met with the advertisement, we sent over to England for the book; it is Dr. Bucknill's " Psychology of Shakespeare." The acumen, the modesty, the enthusiasm, and the judgment which mark every page of this delightful work, have rendered it a real acquisition to us Shakespeare-lovers. So charmed is my husband with it, that after reading it aloud to me, he is going through it again to himself. A greater compliment can hardly be paid to a work than a second perusal immediately upon a first. Most striking it is, to perceive how each new writer upon Shakespeare, professionally versed and interested in one especial branch of learning, thinks that the poet of poets must have made that particular branch his especial study. Rushton and L. Campbell think he must have been a lawyer; a military man writes an article to prove that he must have served as a soldier; a naval captain protests that he must have been a sailor; and now a superintendent of a lunatic asylum shows cause why he must have made brain-diseases his peculiar investigation. Glorious privilege of matchless genius! It makes its own all that it touches; and it forces the conviction upon those best qualified to judge in the several subjects they are conversant with, that it must have laboured in those knowledges which it acquires by its own force of penetration.

Hoping that you and yours have enjoyed good health and all prosperity this summer, and may long continue to do so, I am

Your affectionate
MARY COWDEN CLARKE.

Charles joins me in kindest wishes and regards.

TO ROBERT BALMANNO; SURNAMED
MY ENTHUSIAST AND FATHER-IN-LOVE

My dear Enthusiast! well does that name
  Express the fervour and the hearty glow,
  The Highland warmth of feeling, never slow
To greet with kindly sympathy the flame
Of worthy effort ; genially it came,
  In frank outpouring and unstinted flow
  On one who never could have dream'd to know
From unknown friend such cordial and untame
  Approval ; constant, steady, staunch regard ;
A love parental, partial, and content
To like in spite of faults; for aye intent
  On keeping vigilantly watch and ward
O'er all the interests and vantage-gain
That may an honouring renown maintain :
  Enthusiastic friendship such as this,
  Forms rarest privilege and meek-proud bliss ;
It kindles an enthusiasm in return,
Whose flame of grateful ardour ever more will burn.

June 8th, 1859.

NICE, NOV. 9, 1859.

MY DEAR ENTHUSIAST:

I WRITE to acknowledge the due receipt of yours, dated Oct. 14, 1859, sent through 69 Dean St., London; and also to tell you that we are going for change of air for a month or so, Charles having felt not well lately, and Alfred having planned a charming excursion to Parma, Modena, Bologna, Florence, and Sienna. Our party is to consist of Alfred, Clara, Sabilla, Charles, and myself, — all fine lovers of family-travelling and picture-seeing. We take our driver Pasquale and his roomy coach, which will just hold us, our carpet-bags, and our four "green books;" which latter, darling Clara stipulated for, knowing my thirst for music and her voice, together with my delicacy in asking her to sing unoffered on her part. Let me whisper in your ear: Charles has a scheme, which he means to put in train on our return from our trip, for obtaining a note from Harriet Martineau that he may send it to you. I am unable to tell you her address; but I should fancy that if you were to direct a letter to her, care of her publisher, it would be safely forwarded.

How you interested me with your description of your curious dream! This climate makes me dream most vividly and continually; when

it does not exercise its usual sleepless effect,
it causes active dreaming, and you would be
entertained, could you know the pertinacious
way in which my dream-thoughts paint and
re-paint past scenes and persons of my life.
Alfred will add a line on the last page of this;
and as I have several letters to write, and pack-
ing-up to accomplish, I will bid you good-bye,
praying you to excuse this brief letter. But
however short, I *would* write it before I went
away, to bid you good-bye till my return, and to
repeat — what you know by heart by this time,
but which I also know you like to know again
and again — that I am faithfully

Your attached daughter-in-love,

MARY COWDEN CLARKE.

Our united affectionate love to dear Mrs.
Balmanno.

NICE, JAN. 2, 1860.

MY DEAR ENTHUSIAST:

AMONG my first duties in commencing
another New Year is to write to you; and
having lately dispatched a heap of Shakespeare
proofs, I am left free to fulfil this duty, which is
also a pleasure. I wrote to you last, Nov. 9, to
tell you of the delightful journey then in prospect. It proved as delightful in fact. Our

original programme included Parma, Modena, Bologna, and Sienna as well as Genoa and Florence; but as the snow made its appearance on the mountains, we thought it more prudent not to venture among them, so confined ourselves to the beautiful coast road where the sun shone and the rain kept off. It was curious to see the latter clinging to the uplands, while we jogged along in clear weather, which was an essential to our enjoyment, since Alfred occupied the box seat, and would have been wet through had rain fallen. Oh, my dear sir, it was a charming time! Trudging on with my dear men-folk, when the coach stopped for its noon-tide repose; saturating our eyes with the beauties of that famed Riviera road, the celebrated "Cornice," now looking down precipitous cliffs draped with olive trees, to the blue Mediterranean beneath; now looking up to heights crowned with the same silvery foliage; now coming to some picturesque town perched on an isolated eminence; now crossing a torrent that poured down through some green valley flanked by undulating slopes; now sitting by the roadside to discuss our lunch of bread and dried fruits, or a batch of home-made gingerbread that Clara had not only brought with her for us, but had made with her own hands; now waiting for

the coach to overtake us, and getting in to have
an animated chat with the two insides, Clara and
Sabilla, the former of whom especially is always
ready with a flow of the most lively, entertaining, original-viewed, and sprightly-expressed talk
imaginable. Once she enchanted us with a
verse or two of Scotch song; and another time,
with a strain from Himmel,[1] and "O Salutaria,"
that she knows is one of my choicest favourites.
It stirs my inmost soul; and as her voice pours
it forth, I feel as if an angel were quiring to me,
and giving me a glimpse of heaven. She ami-
ably insisted on our bringing with us our "green
books" containing our unaccompanied vocal
music; and one evening at Florence, we had
some of our old favourites. These things combine to make me feel as if old times were returned to gladden my heart again. I went with
her to high mass in the Cathedral at Pisa, and
during the offertory the organist played a beautiful piece of harmony, which was indeed welcome to my ears. For you must know that the
majority of organ music now played in Italian
churches is the most offensively *unsacred* possible. During this service I chose my station
where my eyes could rest upon a divine "St.

---

[1] Friedrich Heinrich Himmel, a German composer, died 1814.

John," by Andrea del Sarto, an exquisite picture. At Pisa also, in one of the palaces there, we were fortunate enough to make the acquaintance of a magnificent painting by Guido Reni, one of the largest specimens of the master I have ever seen, and proportionately grand, — fine colouring and masterly drawing. We renewed our loving knowledge of our darlings at Florence, in the Uffizi and Pitti galleries, besides regaling our eyes with some curious ancient pictures in the Accademia delle Belle Arte there. I paused, with breathless reverence, in front of the large padded door which opens into the tribuna; and when I entered, one of my first acts was to waft a kiss, in your name, to the presiding beauty of the room, your adored Venus de' Medici. You may be sure I did not omit repairing to the one room there, hallowed to me by such dearly-treasured memories, the Hall of Niobe. As I sat in the chair I had seen her occupy when I first found her seated there, the intervening time seemed a blank, and I felt restored to her in spirit. How often I am so in my dreams at night, is strange.

Accept yourself, my dear sir, the sincere attachment of

MARY COWDEN CLARKE.

LETTERS TO AN ENTHUSIAST

NICE, APRIL 10TH, 1860.

MY DARLING ENTHUSIAST:

YOU have of course seen the Christmas number of Charles Dickens's "All the Year Round," — "The Haunted House." I admire the first story extremely for its grace and sweet taste; I think the garden-room story very clever; Master B.'s charms me with its quaint humour and feeling of pathos beneath; and the poem-story was to me exquisite.

The other day, the veteran vocalist, Tamburini — who is here with his family this season, and who preserves his glorious voice and finished style of singing wonderfully well — offered Clara to come and sing with her some duets for a few of our friends, who wished of all things to hear them together. Such a treat as this musical morning did not fail to get whispered about; and several of those persons who had previously had invitations to Charles's lectures obtained Alfred's invitation to this musical feast: among others, our charming Princess[1] and her delightful, truly German husband, good-humoured and easy in the extreme, and also his highness, the Prince of Oldenburg, who is a great lover of music. Expecting these royalties, we of course

---

[1] Princess Mathilde Reuss Koestritz.

placed a front row of armchairs for their high-
nesses, in the centre of which the American
Chair was stationed. But when the Princes and
the Princess arrived, neither of them would occupy the grand throne-chair; and we had the
experience of seeing the dumb-show of defer-
ence that took place, — the Prince of Oldenburg
bowing and signing to the Princess Reuss
Koestritz to take the place of honour as being
the lady, while she curtseyed and waved to him
to take it as being of the higher rank. Finally,
they each took a seat beside the American
Chair, leaving it empty between them, as far too
grand for either of them to occupy.

You would, I know, admire our Princess; she
is so sweet-natured, so unaffectedly gracious and
kind, so cheerful, so beaming-eyed, so every-way
enchanting. I can't keep my eyes off her delightful face, whenever she is here; and she, in
turn, keeps hers fixed on my Charles the whole
time he is speaking, and evidently adores his
lecturing. This, you will say, perfectly accounts
for my adoration of her.

You ask whether "Nice is on the small island
of Sardinia, or in Sardinia in Italy." And then
you add: "If Nice and Savoy are annexed to
France, will you be annexed? Pray say, for I
am bothered." Ah, my dear sir, this annexation

question has been a perfect botheration to us all.
I, for my part, am heartsick about it; what with
utter repugnance to the thought of being handed
over to France, to live under the rule of an arch-
liar,[1] to be under French government, and what
with the nausea of hearing the topic constantly
and angrily discussed, I feel thoroughly worn
out with the subject. The Count, I feel assured,
will never submit to live under French domina-
tion, therefore the Gigliuccis will certainly remove, should Nice no longer be Italian; Sabilla
is a red-hot Italy-woman, and Alfred has adopted
the partisanship; so all these things go to give
a likelihood of our leaving here for a domicile
farther south. We shall see. Meantime I teach
my soul what patience it can practise, and endeavour to acquire a liking for whatever I find
the majority of our family-party prefer.

I find I have forgotten, after all, to answer
your query relative to the position of Nice. It
is not on the island of Sardinia, but is in Sardinia in the Sardinian states; is about five miles
from the Pont du Var, — the French frontier,
— and forms the point of coast to the extreme
east of the long south line occupied by Provence
between Marseilles and this place. As long as
I can, [I will] continue to date Nice, Sardinia;

---

[1] Napoleon III.

when it is no longer Sardinian, but French, I shall put simply " Nice Maritime," which is sufficient for postal purposes.

Good-bye. God bless you and yours!

MARY COWDEN CLARKE.

NICE, MAY 30TH, 1860.

MY DARLING ENTHUSIAST :

I RECEIVED your kind letter of the 14th April, announcing that you had sent me off the requested first number of our edition of Shakespeare to Dean St. I heard of the name of the Italian Shakespeare, Crollolanza, from my brother-in-law, Count Gigliucci. I find that Crollolanza is a Turinese, and a living writer, but I believe, of not great eminence; there is certainly not as much similitude between the two renowns as between the two names.

Nice is fast lapsing into its summer solitude. The season is over; the strangers — English, Russians, and Germans — are taking flight, and the streets are deserted. Tradespeople look at you as if you must be demented, if you inquire for articles only to be had during the influx of visitors, and coolly tell you you must wait till next October if you expect to find any such thing in all the town. The heats have not yet set in; indeed the weather is still remarkably

cool for Nice at this period of the year. Alfred
has not left for any tour, so he takes us out for
evening drives, which are truly delightful. We
go to the valley of St. Andre, the romantic spot
I mentioned to you some time since in one of
my letters; but the nightingales are not in great
force this year: too cool, I fancy, for those warmth-
loving little creatures. I enjoy the freshness, and
find it suits me in health; for I am very well just
now, thank God.

All my family unite with Charles and myself
in kindest remembrances to you and Mrs. Balmanno; and hoping soon to have news from you
that both she and you are still in the same good
health you were when last you wrote, I am

Your affectionate

MARY COWDEN CLARKE.

NICE MARITIME, JUNE 22ND, 1860.

MY DEAR ENTHUSIAST:

HOW you would have been charmed, could
you have witnessed the little scene that
took place here this morning! Clara and her
two darling girls came and sang a trio of Men-
delssohn, and one of Cherubini, under our window at a quarter to six (the very hour and minute
at which I was born half a century ago), in cele-

[303]

bration of the day. Could you have heard those
fresh young voices, mingled with one no whit less
fresh and clear, in that exquisite music, with the
still morning air, and the garden quietude; and
when Charles threw open our east window, to
behold those dear, loving faces looking up at us
with smiles of affectionate joy and mirth, their
rosy cheeks and bright eyes vying with the
beauty of the flowers that filled to overflowing
a basket which the two girls held between them,
you would have said a lovelier combination of
sound and sight was rarely, if ever, beheld.
You may readily imagine the effect it had on
my heart and imagination; and when they came
trooping up into our room to embrace us both, I
kissed them through a shower of happy tears.

Dear Clara does indeed bring up her children
well, entering into all their pleasures, and giving
them endless innocent gaieties, cultivating their
affections and intellects, and taking part in all
their childhood pursuits. She and her husband
truly deserve to be parents, so admirably do
they fulfil the sacred character and comprehend
its duties. Their boys and girls will, doubtless,
turn out just such men and women as best form
a father's and mother's reward.

They are all about to repair for the summer
season to the Baths of St. Didier, not far from

Mont Blanc. Thence they will go on to Paris,
and finally to England, the family accompanying
Clara thither this year in her visit for the autumn provincial festivals, as a delightful treat
for them all. It is probable that Alfred will go
at the same time, taking Sabilla with him for
the holiday; and a charming one they will be
sure to enjoy. I must tell you of a delightful
day we lately had. Alf took a carriage, with our
favourite driver, Pasquale, to a Provençal village
called Vence, about ten or twelve miles from
here; himself, Clara, Sabilla, Charles, and myself forming the party. We found an enchanting spot, where we sat under a noble oak tree,
to discuss our noontide repast. Near to us
were a grand old spreading Spanish chestnut,
a shady walnut tree, and groups of olive trees.
At our feet lay a sloping green bank, which
ended in a rapid, rocky-bottomed streamlet,
overgrown with copsewood, in which sang a
nightingale. Up from the rivulet stretched
a verdant foreground, terminating in some fine
bold crags, on one of which sat perched a picturesque town. In the extreme distance to the
right lay Nice and her line of gray mountains;
while toward the south was just visible the broad
placid blue of the Mediterranean. It was a glorious landscape; and, as our eyes feasted on it, I

had the pleasure of reading aloud to my dear
companions Charles Dickens's last "Uncom-
mercial Traveller," containing those delicious
descriptions of my darling old fields and lanes
of beautiful Kent and Surrey.

Another memorable holiday I lately enjoyed.
Alf and I got up at two o'clock in the morning,
sallied out, alpenstock in hand, and shod with
our stout mountain boots, climbed the crag lying
to the east of our house, the full moon shining
blandly, and the fireflies flitting about by hundreds. We had no sooner reached the summit
than the faint light of dawn saluted our eyes in
the Orient. I sat and watched it, while Alf found
a nook in an old ruined mill that crowns the
ridge, kindled the fire, and heated some coffee
that we had brought with us. In face of the glorious spectacle of the rising sun, we sipped our cup
of hot coffee and munched our crust of bread. In
front was the mountain-rock of Turbia, with its
ruined remains of a Roman tower backed by the
golden sunrise; the sea was sparkling with the
level rays, and showing the outline of land that
indicates where the island of Corsica lies, and
which is only to be descried from here at sunrise or sunset. To our left was the Fort of
Mont Alban on the near height, beyond which
rose the loftier range, surmounted in the distance

by the snowy peaks of the Finistre Mountains.
The moon paled as the sun rose; and we returned to breakfast when the hour was still
so early that it enabled us to laugh at those lie-
abeds, Sabilla and Charles, who preferred staying at home and called ours a mad excursion. I
can only say that, to my thinking,

> " No settled senses of the world can match
> The pleasure of that madness." [1]

I have left only room to wish myself many
happy returns of the day that may include the
pleasure of being able to write to my dear
Enthusiast and tell him how truly I am his

Affectionate

MARY COWDEN CLARKE.

NICE MARITIME, JULY 15TH, 1860.

MY DARLING ENTHUSIAST :

I DID not acknowledge the receipt of your
delightful letter of the 6th and 18th June
(which arrived, charmingly, on our wedding day,
July 5th) until to-day, as I knew you would like
me to write on a date sanctified to us as this
is by a certain book and chair. Your quips
about " Crollolanza " were very pleasant and

---

[1] " Winter's Tale," Act V, Scene III.

most kindly ingenious. Thanks for enclosing me the copies of them.

You ask me if I ever heard of, or read, "Uncle Tom's Cabin." I have laughed over it, wept over it, honoured it, and had a copy of it, since the first moment I knew of its valued existence. Thank you for telling me of the whereabouts of its admired authoress. Be assured I will not fail to call and offer my most sincere homage, if I should learn that Mrs. Beecher Stowe is in Nice.

Our Princess is an English lady married to a German Prince, and yet another than the darling you imagine. Our Princess is the Princess Mathilde Reuss Koestritz, and is called "Our Princess" by us because we all love and admire her so particularly. Did I tell you that when she left Nice I had the pleasure of sending her a little silk case embroidered with a group of roses, pansies, and forget-me-nots, enclosing two sonnets I wrote in remembrance of a delightful evening's conversation Charles and I had with her highness, when she did us the pleasant honour to find us out in a nook where we had quietly ensconced ourselves, at a large party given by a distinguisded Scotch lady here, last winter? This — the Hon. Mrs. Archibald Cochrane's — and one to which our Princess invited us — both ladies making a point of desiring our

company — were the only parties we two quiet-
est of quiet folk could resolve upon going to.
But we could not resist the kind insistings of
two such women, so amiable in character, so high
in rank. You should have seen your simple
little daughter-in-love at the Princess's soirée.
The richest and most tasteful toilets; the most
gorgeous jewels, a perfect blaze of diamonds;
Princes, Excellencies, Marquises, and Counts,
with stars on their breasts and whole rows of
orders on their coats; and ladies, few without a
title; while your quiet little daughter and her
husband were called upon every moment to bow
and curtsey, presented by our Princess to some
highness, grace, or ladyship, who had heard of
the gentleman who gave such interesting lectures
on Shakespeare, — a wonder and novelty at
Nice, where intellectual pleasures are rarest of
the rare.

Your picturesque dream was indeed charming, and charmingly described. It recalls our
dear and honoured Douglas Jerrold's delightful
fancy of the fruit-and-bill woman on the " Shakespeare Night " in No. 335 of " Punch." Certainly
one of the most exquisite compliments ever paid
to woman, and inestimably prized by me; so
exactly in dear Jerrold's own playful style! Do
you remember it, father-in-love?

Our family party have all flown. The Gigliuccis — the Count, Clara, and their four children
— are gone to Switzerland, for the Baths of St.
Didier, during the summer; then to Paris, then
to London. Alfred took Sabilla for a tour of
some length to Turin, Germany, England, where
he will remain a week or two; then back to the
continent, and so on by the Danube to Turkey,
visiting Constantinople, Athens, Sicily, on their
way home to Nice. Before he went, he kindly
planned a little trip for Charles and myself,
which we much enjoyed, to see Grasse and
Cannes; the former place being famous for
its flower-growing, and perfume-distillery, and
scented-soap-making.

Ever your gratefully affectionate

M. C. C.

NICE MARITIME, AUG. 14TH, 1860.

MY DEAR ENTHUSIAST:

WE fancied you would like to have this
portrait of the place we live in, and be
able thoroughly to picture to yourself our present
domicile. The grounds in which the house
stands, with the environments and background
of olive woods and mountain heights, are all
accurately rendered, and the whole effect faithfully conveyed. The two windows in the corner

— the one with the lower blind a little raised, and the other with half the blind put back — are the ones belonging to our room. Charles was sitting writing behind the former, I behind the latter, while the photograph was being taken. The window next — with the blind wholly open showing the toilet glass within — belongs to the room occupied by Sabilla; the next — with the two lower blinds raised — is belonging to my father's room; and the last south window, with the one looking west, belongs to Alfred's room. The circle in front, surrounded by the climbing plants (a Banksia rose, interspersed with scarlet geranium and plumbago) is a sundial, bearing the inscription, " Conto soltanto le ore serene." I took this pretty motto from a passage in one of Shelley's books, where he speaks of having met with it in an Italian garden, and gives it in English : " I mark only the bright hours." Beneath the sundial are the two parlour windows ; and to the right of them — beneath our south window — is the entrance door, which stands above a flight of steps leading on to a small trellised terrace, not well seen in the picture. The vine-trellised approach to the house, too, is not very clearly made out; but it is indicated, on the extreme left, leading up to the front court, beneath the parlour windows. Clara's house does

not come into the view; but it lies to the extreme
right, on a level with and beyond the white house
that appears there. The long white patch in
the middle, on the left side, is a new road they
are making; a raised embankment through some
neighbouring grounds. The white house in the
middle distance beneath the mountains is Miss
Bird's — the lady whose history is supposed to
have furnished the groundwork of Charles
Dickens's Christmas Tale of " The Battle of
Life." The building on the summit of the
eastern height is Fort Mont Alban; and the
distant mountain in the centre is Mont Luze,
along the side of which the famous Cornice road
to Genoa passes, at an immense elevation above
the sea. When you read this description, with
the copy of the photograph before you, you will,
I hope, be able to trace out satisfactorily our
whereabouts.

Dear Clara often writes to me, sending lively
accounts of her and her husband's and children's
present sojourn among the Alps. She has, with
her own energetic activity, been learning lace-
making of the Swiss peasants about her; and
between whiles, there being no pianoforte in the
little out-of-the-way village where they are staying for the benefit of its baths and waters, she
has been learning the new music she has to

sing at the autumn festivals in England this next season by the aid of a tuning-fork merely. To quote you her own characteristic words, she says in her last letter to me: " I have managed to learn my 'Armida' all but by heart with a pitch-fork, — musically used, not agriculturally, — which, though troublesome, when once so learned remains more firmly than with any sort of accompaniment." So like Clara; practical and alert-minded, thinking no trouble too much to acquit herself thoroughly well before the public in her own beautiful art. It seems almost a pity they should lose so fine a vocalist, in the very prime of her powers, too; but she right now has to devote herself to her husband and children, at the very period of life when the latter most need her personal maternal care. Charles and I join in heartiest assurances of grateful attachment to yourself and Mrs. Balmanno, begging you ever to think of me as

Your affectionate

MARY COWDEN CLARKE.

NICE MARITIME, OCT. 16, 1860.

MY DEAR ENTHUSIAST:

AFTER a particularly agreeable few days here together, hearing news of dear old England and English friends, and seeing all the

pretty English things they have brought thence,
they left yesterday morning, cosily seated in the
coupé of the diligence, which they had to themselves. When we had seen them off (provided
with a dainty packet of sandwiches, which I got
up early to prepare for them with my own hands,
—as they particularly affect my sandwiches,—
and a heap of letters and papers brought by
the London post just in time for their starting),
Charles and I went to call upon a sweet young
lady friend, an American born, married to a
young doctor who is settled here. You should
have seen the artless joy that lighted up her
gentle countenance when I took her a little
morisco jacket from Sabilla, as a remembrance
gift, I having made it up. She, with genuine
grace, put it on at once, that I might see how
well it fitted; and a most pretty picture she
made, as she sat there, her glowing cheeks and
sparkling eyes setting off the rich brown and
gold of the jacket. Her brother-in-law—the
clever artist, Louis Desanges, who has been
painting the series of spirited portraits that
compose the Victoria-Cross Gallery in London
—ought to have been present to have made a
sketch of her on the spot, she would have formed
so lovely a subject for a painting. Afterwards,
the day being supremely calm, we made the

faithful Pasquale drive us out into the country, to some beautiful copse-woods beyond a perched-up village called Cagnes (not Cannes, where Lord Brougham's seat is), and there we sat enjoying our lunch of fruit, — grapes and rosy apples, — and wandering about, gathering ferns and myrtles, which grow in profusion there. These, on our return, we arranged in vases, and charming they look. I enclose one for you to see; and I know you will view it with added interest when I tell you that I have taken it from a basket that came from honoured Florence Nightingale's sick-room.[1] When Sabilla was in London she went to see her, and took her a copy of the "Notes on Nursing," which Sabilla has translated into Italian. Noble Miss Nightingale was very ill; but she rallied sufficiently to accept the offer which Sabilla and dear Clara made her that the latter would sing for her. After the songs, with the instinct of a graceful mind, Miss Nightingale's devoted cousin and nurse, Miss Carter, filled a basket from the side of Florence's sofa with flowers, and gave it to our darling, in her gratitude for the heavenly music she had just uttered. I tell you this be-

---

[1] A leaf, carefully pressed, selected from this basket, was in this letter, just as it had been placed there by Mrs. Clarke's hand.

cause I know it will interest you, as it did me, I cannot say how much. With a generosity that filled me with proud joy, Clara and Sabilla both agreed that I ought to possess this hallowed basket; and it now adorns our parlour here.

We hope to see all our dear travellers back here toward the end of next month, the Count, Clara, and their children from the North, Alfred and Sabilla from the South.

With our united kindest regards to Mrs. Balmanno and yourself, believe me to be, my dear sir,

Your affectionate
MARY COWDEN CLARKE.

NICE MARITIME, DEC. 13, 1860.

MY DEAR ENTHUSIAST:

THANK you very much for your welcome note of the 30th October. We are here in all the uncertainties of a compelled change of domicile. The former proprietor of this ground has just sold it; and according to Continental law, it seems that a sale of an estate affects a lease thereon; consequently the lease granted to us of this house does not hold good, and we are liable to be turned out by the new proprietor. The Niciard style of procedure is that which may fairly come under the denomination of dirty; therefore you may imagine we are somewhat perplexed. Singularly enough, just at this juncture, an estate near here which has long been an object of Alf's desire was offered him for sale; and though the price was exorbitant, he at once made the purchase. The situation of this estate, its view, its air, its water, its soil, are all superexcellent, but its house is a nest of cupboards, in the usual Nice style. This would necessitate building a new dwelling-house, and Alf has already made a charming design for one. Now, however, "the rub." The Gigliuccis cannot think of staying here under the new order of things, and the whole family have to remove soon into Italy. The Count has already placed his two boys in college at Genoa, and Clara and he are just gone thither, to see for a house there that will suit them.

You may readily fancy that the loss of themselves and their dear children as neighbours is a dreadful drawback to us. Accordingly, Alfred hesitates to begin building; and moreover, when he and Sabilla were at Genoa in November, they saw a property which they fell in love with there. So strong a fancy did Alf take to this place that he wished Charles and me to go and look at it, in hope that we should find it as attractive for a future domicile as he did. Well,

we four took flight on the second, for a week's
trip to Genoa. A more singular spot than the
one Alf had pitched upon it has never been my
fortune to behold. I was extremely interested
with it, and I could see how, to one of his faculty
in perceiving the capabilities of a place, it had so
powerfully fascinated him. Nevertheless, the
present proprietor and he did not come to terms;
and we returned to Nice with nothing definitely
settled. The journey back was curiously in
keeping, so to say, with the peculiarity of the
place we had been to see. The place was like a
place in a book, so odd, so picturesque in the view
it commanded, so altogether strange in itself;
while the journey back was one of the most wild
and wonderful that can be imagined. No one
who has not witnessed the effect of rainy weather
— continuously rainy weather — in these moun-
tainous districts can form any idea of the marvels produced on the Cornice road by many
days' pouring rain. Precipitous rocks, with every
point a water-spout; roaring sea-waves dashing
up from beneath, as if to drag us down and over-
whelm us; water-courses swollen into torrents,
tearing across the road with fearful rapidity and
depth; masses of stone, earth, and trees hurled
across the highway and blocking up the passage,
were the chief features of the scene. Once we

had to get out of the diligence, while the horses were taken from the traces, and the coach was pushed by men over a steep and narrow mule-bridge in the dark; another time, it was let down by ropes and eased along a sharp declivity like the side of a house, while we stood on the opposite bank under umbrellas, watching the descent of the lumbering vehicle. One night we had to stop until the waters of an impassable torrent had subsided sufficiently to let us safely ford it; another night we had to sleep on the road, while the *cantonniers* dug out a passage for the diligence through a heap of rock, stones, and earth, as huge as two large houses, which had fallen across the road only two hours previously. All these perils were bad enough as long as we had daylight; but when darkness came on, and we had to make our way along a ledged road many hundred feet above the sea, liable at any moment to be buried beneath falling masses of earth, or overflowed by rapid torrent waters, it became rather nervous work. My imagination was so powerfully appealed to by all these unwonted incidents that it strove and toiled beyond all power of sleep; and I could only strain my eyes through the murky obscurity of pouring rain and objects dimly seen by the diligence lamps, in heartbeating excitement. After thirty hours of deferred arrival beyond our due time, we reached Nice in safety, thank God, on the evening of the 9th; much, as you may believe, to the relief of dear Clara and our expectant friends.

With abundance of affectionate wishes for many Merry Christmases and Happy New Years to yourself and dear Mrs. Balmanno, from all our family circle, believe me to be

Your attached

Mary Cowden Clarke.

Nice Maritime, 14th June, 1861.

My dear Enthusiast :

ALF writes us word that his alterations in Villa Novello at Genoa are proceeding satisfactorily, so far as substantiality is concerned, but more slowly than could be wished. However, " Slow and sure " is an acknowledged good motto; therefore let us hope that it will be illustrated in the present instance. Clara has been trying to obtain a place nearer our quarter of the city, — Carignano quartière, — as the Count only took the house they now occupy for a year. But it seems the houses and apartments all let well in the neighbourhood of our villa; which shows that it is an

excellent one, although not particularly fashionable. The more suited to us who, one and all, prefer comfort and quiet to gentility.

Nice has now subsided into its usual state of summer void: all the season visitors gone, streets deserted, shops all but closed, lodgings empty! When we occasionally drive through the town, our carriage looks like a solitary ghost of all the gay equipages that throng the thoroughfares during the winter and early spring. Pasquale's whip sounds like an echoing lonely smack, and the horses' hoofs trample along with a kind of spectral reverberations — a faint reminiscence of equine cavalcades and clamour.

I had a long and very interesting letter from Mrs. Farrar by yesterday morning's post-delivery. She gives a most animated account of the judicious proceedings of the North men, ay, and of the North women too. God send that this struggle in America may result in showing "the soul of goodness in things evil"![1]

Charles has lately had sent him a present, Miss Martineau's "Eastern Life, Present and Past," and he has been reading it aloud to me as I

---

[1] "There is some soul of goodness in things evil,
Would men observingly distil it out."
— "King Henry V," Act IV, Scene I.

work, both deriving great pleasure therefrom.
Not only is the subject interesting, but the way
in which she treats it renders it doubly so. The
perusal of this book makes me hope more than
ever that we may some day meet with the one
you mentioned, on Egyptian travel, as containing so much interest for you and Mrs. Balmanno
when you read it together.

Did you see the account of that wonderful
German wiseacre's book which he calls a " Key
to Shakespeare's Sonnets," wherein he propounds,
as a solution to the enigma which has hitherto
puzzled the commentators, namely, who the letters W. H. stand for (to whom the Sonnets are
dedicated), that these initials are to be inter-
preted — William himself! Henceforth, I think,
the title " Mr. William Himself," discovered by
this sapient German, may fairly rank with the
Frenchman's cognomen of " the immortal Williams." I own I am curious to see this German's
" Key," if it be only to find out how he accounts
for the *Mr.* in the dedication.

I must tell you something that made us
smile the other day. I think I mentioned to
you my peasant-pupil, a young girl whom I go
and hear read every morning, and teach to write
and cast accounts, and whom Clara requested
me to take in hand when she left for Genoa. A

regular Italian peasant-girl — warm, brown complexion, jet-black hair and eyelashes, dark eyes, and white teeth. It is a delight to watch the rich colour of her cheek in the excitement of learning, and to see her agile form and her handsome face peering down at me from the cherry tree she climbs to gather me a basket of the fresh fruit. She is the daughter of the peasants who live on the estate Alf bought here, and who cultivate its ground. She is intelligent, though hitherto wholly untaught; and the other morning, when she was reading to me a story from her book, — which is for the most part free from such tract-like trash, — she came to an account of an odious, model, good boy, who did everything according to virtue-pattern. Among other points, it says that "he ate a good deal of soup at dinner, which he was not fond of, because his parents wished it and because he knew it was good for him." Then the story went on to say that "he never omitted to say grace after meals, and thank God for the things he gave him." Whereupon my peasant-pupil turned her large dark eyes upon me, with an arch smile parting her red lips, and said: "For the *soup*, which he did n't like?" It is curious to note how these unsophisticated natures see at once through conventional shams.

Charles and I write in kindest regards to you and dear Mrs. Balmanno. He hopes you duly received a " Manchester Examiner " he sent you, containing a well-written and pleasant notice of *Our* Shakespeare.

Ever affectionately,

MARY COWDEN CLARKE.

9TH SEPT., 1861,
VILLA NOVELLO, IN CARIGNANO, GENOA.

MY DEAR MRS. BALMANNO:

MOST kind was it of you to write me that letter of the 18th August; and yet what pain its contents gave me you can well imagine. Ah, dear madam, thoroughly does my heart sympathize in the suffering yours must be enduring, to see that dear, kind, cheerful nature quelled by so exhausting a disorder. Like you, however, "I will not imagine that the result will be fatal." My dear father-in-love's fine constitution and temperate habits must surely prevail, and restore him to us again. Meanwhile, bid him to care nothing for being unable to answer my letters, or for failing to remember the meaning of that date, or any other playful trifle I may have alluded to in the old style of pleasantry between us. I undermarked the 15th July as being the day I commenced the Concordance, and the day on which the testimonial chair from America was dated, as presented to his honoured daughter-in-love. God bless him for his many, many

[324]

loving-kindnesses to her, who ever thanks him gratefully in her heart of hearts! Tell him so, dear Mrs.
Balmanno; for I will trust and believe that he is still
with you. Tell him the thought of him and his interest in Genoa was among my strongest ideas on arriving here, and that I will look forward to the pleasure
of receiving his letters here, and of writing him a full
account of our home here. Charles and I were — only
a short time before the advent of your letter — agree-
ing how interested my dear Enthusiast would be in a
minute description of this place, and I was intending
to detail it fully. Tell him how much I thank him for
his present of the book — " Stephen's Travels " —
which you say he so kindly ordered to be sent to Dean
Street, whence I doubt not it will soon be forwarded,
as there is a case there waiting to be despatched soon
to Genoa. It touched me, your mention of his interest about the article by Mr. Grant White in the
" Atlantic Monthly " on Mr. Payne Collier; so like my
Enthusiast's active zest in Shakespearean subjects. A
day or two ago, when Charles and I had the delight of
reading a really fine article on our edition in the " Examiner," one of our first exclamations was: " How
the dear Enthusiast will glory in this appreciation of
his daughter-in-love's work by the first literary authority extant!" Dear friend, I cannot go on writing upon
other matters to you while my mind is full of only one
— our dear Mr. Balmanno's condition. I read and
reread those few words of hope: " Nevertheless, I
cannot imagine that the result will be fatal. The bad
symptoms are quite abated." Bless you for writing

them; they comfort me so much, and help me to bear the dread that besets me. My last letter, 14th Aug., will show you how entirely I am able to enter into your every feeling on this occasion. Oh, the overwhelming dread of loss! the anxious watching for every favourable indication! the merging one's own fears and wishes in the sole desire to alleviate the suffering of the watched beloved! Charles and I join heart and soul in cordial regards and ardent wishes. My brother Alfred is gone to Nice for the final completion of [arrangements for] our removal thither, and we hope to see him again very, very soon. Were he now with us, he would unite in affectionate remembrances.

God bless you and sustain you, dear Mrs. Balmanno, prays fervently

Your gratefully attached
MARY COWDEN CLARKE.

God grant that the next letter from you may be from both you and your other self! I feel as if I *must* have some more of his own kind words under his own hand.

9TH OCT., 1861,
VILLA NOVELLO, IN CARIGNANO, GENOA.

MY DEAR MRS. BALMANNO:

YOUR letter of the 15th Sept., to my brother Alfred, confirming the fatal intelligence predreaded in yours of the 18th Aug., struck me to the heart. My dear " Enthusiast and father-in-love " has so long been to me a vivid reality, though unseen, a true and intimate friend, though unknown, that I cannot yet believe I am never again to see his welcome handwriting, never again to receive those kind and ever fond letters, animated by so much warmth of regard and prodigality of affection. Perhaps no one in the world can so fully sympathize with your loss as myself; for no one has more deep cause to gratefully feel and know his lavish kindness, his generous enthusiasm, his fervour of sympathy, his active zeal on behalf of those in whom he took interest. He fulfilled his own adopted title of " father-in-love " to the letter and in the spirit of the name; and it is not too strong an expression to say that in him I seem to lose another parent. The heart takes refuge in the hope of meeting those we have loved and lost in another higher life; and to see and know hereafter the loving father-in-love whom I never beheld with mortal eyes now serves to enhance the prospect of immortality. As we grow older, the added number of those we revere among the dead makes the thought of death less and less repugnant, and weans us mercifully from this life. God bless and sustain you, my dear Mrs. Balmanno, in this your grievous bereavement, prays, in all truth of sympathy and love,

Your affectionate and grateful
MARY COWDEN CLARKE.

INDEX

INDEX

INDEX

INDEX

103; her dancing, 105; receives copies from Correggio from Mr. Balmanno, 106; criticism on Italian portraits, 108; trip to Nice, 109; finishes "Girlhood of Shakespeare's Heroines," 113; testimonial chair sent from America, 113, 114; shares Mr. Balmanno's letters with her husband, 115; thanks Mr. Balmanno for planning testimonial, 123; sends acknowledgments to subscribers to testimonial, 123, 125, 130; letter from friend in France, 128; receives American edition of "Girlhood of Shakespeare's Heroines," 131; her opinion of Shakespeare's learning, 131; moves from Craven Hill to Porchester Terrace, 133; visit to Cambridge, 134; Collier's opinion of "Concordance," 136; visit to Stratford-on-Avon, 137; habits — perseverance, 137, 139; receives remittance from Mr. Putnam, 138; theory on jealousy, 138; signature to "Concordance," 139; opinion of Bryant's poems, 141; receives letter from Gen. Swift, 142; sketch as "Mrs. Quickly," 143, 144; receives letter from Mr. Allibone concerning "Concordance," 146; favorite flowers, 148; disapproves of vegetable diet, 155; approves of her husband's feminine friends, 153; Mr. Balmanno's opinion of "Quickly" portrait, 153; Mrs. Cowden Clarke's style of dress, 154; inscription on "Quickly" portrait, 154; cannot extend correspondence, 154; receives black walnut box from Mr. Balmanno, 155; receives from him "Truths Illustrated by Great Authors," 155; her views on gifts, 155; her politics, 156; receives cast and inkstand from Mr. Balmanno, 157; admires amateur work, 158; once made her mother's caps, 158; makes her husband's vests, 158; makes frames for portraits, 159; describes visit to Florence, 160–163; opinion of Guercino, 162; and of Titian, 163; compares Guido's Cleopatra with Shakespeare's, 163; New Year's wishes to Mr. Balmanno, 164; wakefulness, 165, 177; receives "Niobe's Daughter" and inkstand from Mr. Balmanno, 166; Christmas puddings, 168; portfolios, 169, 181; on Drury Lane Theatre free list, 172; makes sandwich-cases for her husband, 174; Shakespeare seals, 178; terror of sea-voyaging, 182; views on mediums, 183; receives engravings for "Girlhood of Shakespeare's Heroines" from Mr. Balmanno, 183; Miss Scott makes set of illustrations for "Girlhood of Shakespeare's Heroines," 183; Mrs. Cowden Clarke makes sandwich-cases for Mr. Balmanno, 184; affection for her husband, 185; acting of "Mrs. Quickly" in 1840, 186; attends Philharmonic rehearsal, 189; handkerchiefs embroidered by her for Countess Gigliucci, 190; idolatry for her family, 190; Countess Gigliucci brings Mrs. Cowden Clarke lace mantilla from Spain, 192; Mrs. Cowden Clarke's delight in acting, 193; views on dancing, 197; admiration for Rachel's acting, 199; silver anniversary, 202; accompanies the Gigliuccis to see German players in "Faust," 203; Countess Gigliucci brings her marabou feathers from Portugal, 206; Mrs. Cowden Clarke joins in singing four-part Thanksgiving composed by her father, 207; trip to Nice, 207; remonstrates with Mr. Balmanno for vexation, 210; asks him to find American publisher for "The Iron Cousin," 215; introduces Mr. Routledge

INDEX

INDEX

INDEX

INDEX

RACHEL, Mrs. Cowden Clarke's opinion of, 54; her acting, 199; notice of, in Boston paper, 246; appearance, 247

Racine, quotation from, 30; Rachel's acting in "Les Horaces," 200; in "Bajazet," 246

"Recollections of Writers," by Mr. and Mrs. Cowden Clarke, 10

Record, 30

"Repose," by Gentileschi, 250

"Retired from Business," by Jerrold, 78

Reuss Koestritz, Princess Mathilde *See* Koestritz, Princess Mathilde Reuss

Reynolds's portrait of Mrs. Siddons, 94, 212

Richardson, Samuel, quotations from, 70, 120; Mrs. Clarke's admiration for, 92

Richter, Jean Paul, his face, 74; quotation, 166; Life of, 166

"Rimini," portrait of Leigh Hunt in, 281

Riviera road, the "Cornice," 296

"Road to Ruin," Munden in, 71

"Robert le Diable," Meyerbeer's, Countess Gigliucci's singing in, 189

Roll, Misses, 35, 70

Roubiliac, Louis François, 253

Routledge, Mr., introduced to Mr. Balmanno by Mrs. Cowden Clarke, 217

Royal Academy Exhibition, 83

Rushton on Shakespeare, 292

Russell, Lord William, 111

ST. ANDREW's festival, 117

"St. Cecilia," by Guercino, 162

St. George's Hall, 235

St. Didier, Baths of, Countess Gigliucci's trip to, 304, 310

"St. John," by Andrea del Sarto, 297

"Sancho Panza," quotation from, 211

Sardinia, Queen of, 143

Sarto's, Andrea del, "St. John," 298

"Scarlet Letter," Hawthorne's, comments on, 87

Scotch songs, 111

Scott, Miss, makes illustrations for "Girlhood of Shakespeare's Heroines," 183

Scott, Wallace, 183, 194

Scott, Sir Walter, quotations from, 174, 277

"Sentiments and Similes," 116

Serle, Lydia, visit to Nice, 268

Serle, Mary, 80

Serle, Mrs. Thomas James (Cecilia Novello), 94; visit to Ugbrooke Park, 262; visit to Nice, 268; Italian tour, 270

Shakespeare, Mr. Balmanno's dream about, 23; proposals for monument to, 45; seals, 47; portrait and bust of, 49; cast from monument, 52; bust, 52; copy of monument, 52; portrait in Collier's edition, 52, 65; Kean's acting in, 72; illustrations by Leslie, 84; extra-illustrated copies, 106; nicknames, 111; papers on, sent to Mrs. Cowden Clarke by Mr. Balmanno, 118; Collier's opinion of, 118; Lansdowne edition, 120; Halpin's paper on, 128, 131; Mrs. Cowden Clarke's opinion of his learning, 131; celebration in America, 146; portrait, 147; seals, 178; revival of "Merry Wives of Windsor," by Mr. Burton, 193; Shakespeare Record, 194; Shakespeare festival, 195; Coleridge on Shakespeare, 262; "Barry Cornwall" on, 262; Thomas Campbell's Life of, 262; Dyce's edition, 269; daguerreotype of, sent to Mrs. Cowden Clarke by Mr. Balmanno, 251, 252; labour necessary for editing, 272; Mrs. Cowden Clarke's delight in, 273; seal broken, 288, 289; effect of Shakespeare's versatility, 292; quotations from — *see* names of plays

Shakespeare, Concordance to, by

INDEX

INDEX